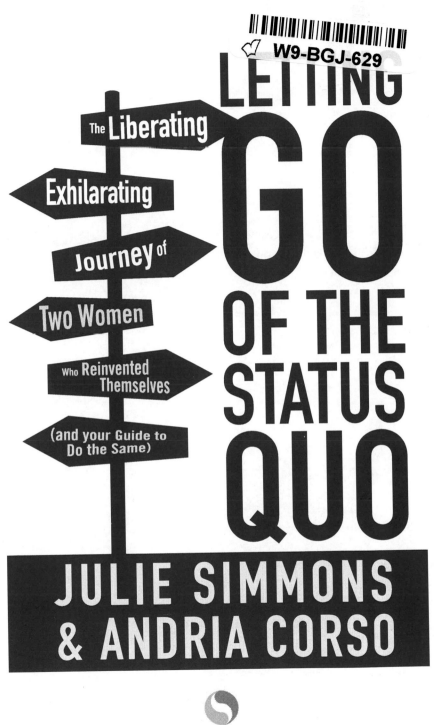

LETTING GO OF THE STATUS QUO

The Liberating

Exhilarating

Journey of

Two Women

Who Reinvented Themselves

(and your Guide to Do the Same)

JULIE SIMMONS & ANDRIA CORSO

Love Your Life

Letting Go of the Status Quo

For more information about this book or the authors, visit:

www.lettinggoofthestatusquo.com

Love Your Life Publishing
www.loveyourlifepublishing.com

ISBN: 978-1-934509-68-5
Library of Congress Control Number: 2012955660
Printed in the United States of America
First Printing 2013

Cover design: www.Cyanotype.ca
Editing by Madeleine Uno and Gwen Hoffnagle
Interior print formatting by Indie Designz

Dedication

This book is dedicated to the many teachers, guides and mentors who helped us along our journey of reinvention. We are humbled to serve as stewards for others who are seeking to let go, look up and find inner peace.

<u>**Status quo** *n.* **The existing condition or state of affairs.**</u>

<u>**—The American Heritage Dictionary**</u>

INTRODUCTION

First, thank you for picking up our book. We are thrilled to be a part of *your* journey. We decided to write this book so we could share our stories about re-creating our lives with other women like you. Having been through significant life changes, and having taken scary and exhilarating risks, we both knew if we could do it, anyone could.

Sometimes the status quo is just what we need. We fit in, we're comfortable, we're making a contribution and feeling connected and alive. But other times we are living by someone else's rules, and that causes constriction. We literally shut down and become outsiders in our own lives. When those feelings surface, it may be time to initiate change—and this book can help you navigate the stages you'll go through.

The two of us were introduced as we were both going through similar shifts in almost every aspect of our lives. Although from the outside our lives looked ideal and rather fortunate, what was going on *inside* was a different story. Initially, Julie felt stuck in her career and sought career counseling from Andria, who had created her new company, C3 Coaching and Consulting, because she felt stymied in *her* corporate career.

Because every part of our lives are intertwined, as we awaken to our true selves, our purpose or our potential in our careers (such as leaving a job that isn't inspiring us or honoring our abilities), this allows us to make changes in personal relationships that are unbalanced, draining us, or may have outlived their initial purpose and vice versa.

We all recognize when our lives are not enough or not what we want them to be—and we *can* change them into the lives of our dreams. We know it is a challenge but we, along with plenty of other women, have successfully navigated this path. Doing this requires letting go of the past (and the present) and stepping boldly into the future. It requires all of the things we both experienced in the chapters that follow (and then some!).

The structure of this book allows us to share two very different stories of how we each let go of the status quo to re-create our lives. We were struck by how many similar stages or what we call "elements" the two of us went through in our separate journeys. Our stories are told within the context of these twelve "necessary elements" or chapters. Each element guided us to step out into the future. First we explain the element, then we tell each of our stories related to that element, and finally we provide Guideposts for our readers to explore their own experiences related to that element.

You will notice that the format of chapters 9 and 10 differs from the others. Chapter 9 contains only "Andria's Story" and Chapter 10 contains only "Julie's story." That is because although our stories overlapped in most elements, they didn't overlap in every area. Each journey towards reinvention is unique. We are two different people with totally different experiences that had many (but not all) common factors.

We truly believe that by sharing our stories we will inspire you to let go of what is not working and create a life that does work—one that allows you to be your most brilliant self.

May you be inspired to experience as exhilarating a journey as we both did—and which we continue to experience! We look forward to hearing about *your* journey and meeting the newly reinvented *you*!

Enjoy!

—Julie & Andria

Table of Contents

CHAPTER 1:
THE STARTING LINE:
IT'S *NOT* OKAY TO JUST BE "OKAY"

The first element is about coming to the realization that your life, as it is today, is no longer working for you. It is the catalyst to begin letting go of the status quo. We found this discovery, that life is no longer okay, to be the platform from which we each re-created our lives. It is both a scary and exhilarating place to be and is an essential and necessary starting point. After all, why would you let it go if it were working for you? You wouldn't; and therefore, acknowledging that you are no longer okay with your life just being "okay" is your wonderful starting line. You are not alone in feeling stuck. Let the journey begin!

—Julie & Andria

Julie's Story

LIVING UP TO MY CAREER POTENTIAL

From all outward appearances my life was great. My husband, Greg, and I had a strong, stable marriage. We traveled extensively, had amazing friends and terrific careers and owned our home. What wasn't visible to others was my struggle to find personal fulfillment. I didn't fit in anywhere. I didn't have children, so couldn't relate to folks who were parents. My job was not challenging, with no options for advancement.

Weren't these supposed to be the best years of my life? Why couldn't I simply embrace the good in my life? Why wasn't I satisfied with the status quo?

There were people who would relish the successes I found in my life, yet I found myself restless and unsatisfied. I couldn't quite put my finger on the reasons, but I kept coming back to the statement, "There must be something more than _this_"—and I set out on a journey to find it.

As I continue my journey to find my Shangri-La, one thing I know for certain is that "okay" is _never_ going to be sufficient for me. I wouldn't trade the lows of my journey if it meant sacrificing the amazing highs. And here is something ironic coming from a type A planner: I wouldn't want someone to tell me what would happen on my journey. Honestly, I wouldn't believe them! I wish I could tell you my journey is extraordinary, but I've learned it isn't. It is, however, unique, with nuggets of strength, optimism and perseverance woven throughout. I decided to share my story because I want other women to know it is worth the investment to reinvent themselves. The reward is priceless.

I'll start with my career reinvention since that is how I met Andria, my amazing co-author, without whom this book wouldn't exist. Andria and I were introduced through a mutual friend and I knew immediately she was special. When you meet Andria you are immediately drawn to her positive energy, confidence and warmth. I knew after our first meeting Andria was someone I wanted to develop a strong relationship with, selfishly, because I felt better after our time together. She is genuine, kind and sincere.

On a sunny fall afternoon Andria gently took me on the first steps of my journey of reinvention without even knowing it. She served as the ideal person for me at a time when I didn't even know I needed a guide. Over our first cup of coffee Andria began to challenge me in ways she instinctively knew I needed. She effortlessly shared stories of her corporate career as well as her decision to start her own business. Within minutes I found myself face to face with someone who shared the exact same feelings, aspirations and vision for living an authentic life. I felt like she was reading my mind. In this meeting I knew Andria was someone who would be instrumental in my life.

As luck would have it (I know now there is no such thing as coincidence) Andria is an executive coach and I was in *serious* need of guidance. I'd been focused on developing my human resources career for fifteen years and didn't know what to do next. Despite having been with my current company for six-and-a-half years, I wasn't seeing the career advancement I was desperate to achieve. My company was incredibly supportive of my desire to continue to find the next professional challenge.

My supervisor provided me with opportunities to expand my network through the local Chamber of Commerce. What started out as a way to market my company turned into a number of deep, meaningful professional relationships. The Chamber enabled me to lead, contribute and learn—all while giving back to the local business community. Little did I know in 2006 how much I would rely on the members of the Chamber to assist me with my professional transition.

But I still wasn't fulfilled at work. With a little hesitation I began to share my feelings with HR colleagues in my professional network. I couldn't articulate what I wanted in a new position and wasn't truly ready to leave my current employer. Over and over again the topic of higher education would come up. Maybe I should get my master's? Many people I worked with had advanced degrees but it really wasn't a necessity in my field. I never considered myself an academic. Getting a master's degree intimidated me and I lacked the confidence in the scholastic arena.

Ultimately I found the courage, thanks to my husband and friends, to enroll in a two-year cohort program at Marymount University. The good thing about my decision to attend graduate school: I knew myself well enough to know what would make me successful—building and nurturing relationships. Once I committed to the program and met the other students, I knew I would finish the program. The fact that I'd found a program structured around a core group of students significantly increased my likelihood of success and completion. Graduate school was a vehicle to scratch my intellectual itch and give me more information to make my next career decision.

I knew the balancing act would be a challenge. I was ready to tackle it.

For two full years my life was consumed with school and work. It wasn't easy and I struggled to find my footing. The academics provided me with an opportunity to stretch and learn more about my chosen field as well as myself. Thanks to outstanding professors and fellow students and interesting reading and project work, I found myself mastering subjects easily. And, before I knew it, I received my M.A. in Human Resources from Marymount University with a 4.0 grade point average.

That's the interesting thing about life; sometimes you simply have to take a risk and trust yourself—you may be surprised when you are suddenly standing where you had only dreamed of being.

Yet, alas, in the fall of 2009, I found myself asking my trusty old stand-by question, "What's next? There must be something more."

While I didn't want to leave my current company, there didn't appear to be an alternative path to advancing my career. I didn't know how to begin a search for a senior level HR position. Yet the process of getting my master's had proved to me that taking a risk can pay off in big ways. I found the confidence in myself and believed I could succeed in a senior level role.

Secretly, I was also considering starting my own boutique HR consulting company. By this time, I'd met Andria, who had a successful business, C3 Coaching and Consulting, and she was willing and able to share her perspectives with me. She encouraged me to take the leap and start my own business. Unfortunately, all I could see were obstacles:

How would I get my first client? How would I market myself? What aspect of human resources would be my focus? Who would pay my bills if I didn't get a client for many months? Aren't we in a recession? This seems like a terrible time to start a business. Half of all small businesses fail in the first year. I had a mortgage to pay. What about health insurance? And how would I fund my retirement account?

So, probably like many of you, I ignored my inner voice and opted to look for a traditional job with a stable company.

Things were definitely okay at work: I loved the people I worked with and had created an amazing team. My work life and home life felt balanced and I'd deepened my philanthropic efforts in the community, something that was increasingly important to me. Yet, despite my best efforts, I was not content.

Every few months I would have the same the inner dialogue: *Are you living up to your fullest potential? What is your next move? How can you continue to grow and develop as a professional? You are capable of more and should be able to showcase your talents on a higher level.* I knew I was short-changing myself. I knew I wasn't going to be content until I found a challenging position.

Finally, I could no longer accept the status quo of staying in a job where I was not fulfilled. Simply existing wasn't how I wanted to live. I was ready, professionally and personally, to take the next step in my career. I wanted to apply the knowledge I had learned in graduate school. Leading a team of professionals was also extremely important to me. I sought an organization that valued my contributions and was in alignment with my personal values. I finally got it: In order to advance my career I would need to leave the safety of my current employer.

First things first.

I am list maker. I love the satisfaction of crossing things off my many lists knowing I've accomplished them. I made a list of the top ten criteria I would need to feel excited and motivated in a new senior-level human resources position.

1. It's headquartered in Northern Virginia
2. Has a progressive approach to HR
3. Females are in leadership positions throughout the company
4. Has a positive reputation in the marketplace
5. Has values that align with my own
6. Supports work/life integration
7. Offers a robust total compensation package
8. Gives me the ability to mentor human resources professionals
9. Has an organizational mission that resonates with me
10. There's a leader or client from whom I can learn

Without a plan I knew it would be difficult to articulate my ideal position. Thanks to the experience I had at the Chamber of Commerce, I knew my professional network would be key to finding the HR leadership position I desired. Armed with my dream job criteria and my updated resume, I began to have conversations with influencers in my professional network.

A seasoned HR professional had recently left my company. She and I were casual acquaintances and I wasn't sure if she would even remember me, but I took a chance and emailed her. I was unaware of her deep presence in the local community of human resources professionals. She had contacts at many well-respected companies near Washington, D.C.

Something I've learned along my journey is people actually want to help other people, and she was no exception. She listened to my dream job criteria list and without skipping a beat, she mentioned a role that seemed like a match at a company locally headquartered in the greater DC area.

The dream job I'd worked for fifteen years to obtain was available and literally within reach. This position met all my criteria. I even had an inside scoop about the team since I was introduced to the opportunity through my professional network. All the stars were aligning! I would not have known about this position had I not taken a risk and contacted my "fairy job mother."

I hadn't interviewed in a number of years, so I fought back butterflies as I dusted off my interview suit. Despite the fact that I work in HR, it is a bit intimidating when you are the candidate. The more I learned about this position, the more excited I found myself. This was going to be an opportunity to apply what I learned in my master's program in a business setting and grow my business acumen in a new industry. As the interview process continued, everything fell into place effortlessly. I had great chemistry with the HR team.

I finally got to the last item on my list: I needed to be comfortable with the leader I'd be supporting or it wasn't going to work for me. Given my strong personal desire to align my values with the organization and leaders I work with, this could be a deal breaker. If he and I didn't see eye to eye, this wasn't going to happen. But within five minutes of meeting him I knew things were going to work out. He was terrific and his leadership style was an exact fit for me. We hit it off immediately.

I walked out of the final interview in October of 2010 as excited and energized as on the first day of school. Giddy with anticipation, I knew I was on the carousel and it was finally my turn to grab the golden ring.

The next week the position was offered to me. I did it. This amazing job was mine! When I started my career I had visualized this exact position; this was the pinnacle I dreamed of achieving. Greg was incredibly supportive and proud of me. Taking the chance, leveraging my network and trusting myself enabled me to change the status quo.

Having the ability to identify what was motivating me and being true to my authentic self helped me leave a role that had become comfortable to take the challenging next step in my career progression. I knew I could no longer ignore my inner voice.

Your reasons for letting go of the status quo are unique to you. Give yourself permission to be different from the crowd. As Dr. Seuss says, "Today you are You, that is truer than true. There is no one alive who is Youer than You."

Truly embracing letting go of the status quo starts with embracing your authentic self. Knowing who you are at the core of your soul is instrumental on this journey of self-reinvention.

Andria's Story:

UNCOUPLING

This is not okay, I thought. There I was, sitting on the edge of my bed, again, sobbing to my best friend, Smith, on the phone. I'd been doing it for years—crying about how unhappy I was in my marriage. Somehow being "not okay" had become normal. Sobbing on the phone to my sister, Debra, had also become normal, but on that wintery Saturday morning, it became crystal clear to me that this, too, was no longer okay.

In between sobs, I was telling Smith that I didn't want to be divorced, *again* (this was marriage number two for me and I was only thirty-five years old). She said very bluntly, "Look, Andria, I respect your desire to be true to your marriage vows and not want another divorce, but you're only thirty-five. Do you really want to live like this *for the rest of your life?*"

I was silent. Not because I didn't know what to say, but because I knew saying the answer out loud would change everything. Finally, I mustered up the strength to respond, "No, I don't want to live like this for the rest of my life." And at that point everything *did* change. Although it took me another six months to actually leave my marriage, in my mind the decision was made that day, sitting on the edge of my cold winter's bed in a suburb of Philadelphia.

Before that fateful day, I had countless other signs that things weren't right in my personal life and needed to change. I woke up many weekends, looked around me and wondered whose life I was living. In many ways it seemed crazy to me, and yet I recognized that I had made the choices and commitments and I was dedicated to honoring them. At the same time, there was still a nudging inside keeping me very unsettled. I now know it was my intuition trying to nudge me to

9

go and live the life I wanted, one designed by me and not by everyone else I was trying to please and seek approval from.

Several years before that Saturday morning, I became tolerant of my marriage and my personal life. I knew I wanted something different but was afraid to do anything about it.

Why? Because I worried about what other people would think: Divorced AGAIN? What a failure. Two failed marriages were too much for me to even think about because it made me feel like a complete disaster. So I ignored it for a long time, and I became complacent. I buried myself in my career. I became so preoccupied with climbing the corporate ladder that, after a while, tolerating my personal life didn't even register with me, until mornings like that Saturday when something happened that opened it all up for me.

Looking back, I realize that all those times of sobbing on the phone were less about the state of my marriage and more about the state of me. I had lost myself in trying to make a marriage (that I knew wasn't right) work. Yet ending it seemed so daunting. I didn't want to hurt my husband and my stepchildren. I didn't want to hurt myself by going through the process of ending our marriage and our life together. We had a life together. It really wasn't THAT bad, was it? Perhaps not, but I knew that morning it was time to stop tolerating something that was less than what I wanted.

My soul was screaming for something more and if I didn't make a change, I'd risk losing myself completely.

At least I still had enough of my identity intact to recognize that I didn't want to live like this for the rest of my life. That answer was the easy part. What came next was a bit more complicated.

The questions flooded my mind: *Who am I outside of this marriage, this relationship that spanned almost a decade of my life? How do I reinvent myself and re-create my life when one of the biggest ways I define it is suddenly gone?* More on that later...

"DE-CORPORATIZING"

Fast-forward two-and-a-half years. I have accomplished a cherished goal, a high-level leadership position in a company where I'd been climbing the corporate ladder for ten years. For most of those years, I loved my job, loved where I worked, and loved what I did for a living.

And then the signs that perhaps I was losing some of that love began to appear; many of them I pushed aside (just as I had compartmentalized my marriage). A big one occurred when I was going to interview for a high-level position that included a promotion I really wanted. The interview and the position were at corporate headquarters. About a week before the interview, I got a phone call from one of my trusted co-workers who was also a mentor and friend. She wanted to share some "feedback" with me about the interview.

This feedback was about the length of my hair. Yes, my long, curly, down-to-the-middle-of-my-back hair was not "corporate headquarters" material. Yes, she was serious. Of course, "they" weren't asking me to *cut* my hair, just to simply pull it back to "fit the image." I remember thinking, *You have got to me kidding me!* But this was no joke.

I brushed it off (no pun intended) and made the decision that, yes, I could pull my hair back and play the role to fit the corporate image. Despite how unsettling it felt, I ignored it and kept my eye on my goal. And yes, I got the job. The following signs were a bit subtler, increasing in intensity about a year after I won the promotion. The environment was very political and I was uneasy about playing politics. I did not want to play games; I just wanted to get my job done. But getting the job done involved playing politics. I hated it. But I pushed those feelings aside and learned to play along.

Stress took its toll. I spent the better part of an entire year sick—nothing serious, thankfully, but just a constant battle with bronchitis, the flu, sinus infections, fevers and viruses. I remember being at work more than once that year with a fever. Looking back, I wonder what the heck I was doing going in to work when I was that sick, but obviously I was not thinking clearly. I was on autopilot.

That same year, after running a huge talent review meeting with the CEO and his staff (during the bronchitis period), my boss told me she needed to give me some feedback. I assumed it would be some constructive feedback on how I could improve running those meetings in the future. Wrong.

She told me that at the start of the meeting when I was reaching across the boardroom table to hand out some materials, my suit jacket and shirt rode up a bit and she could see the tattoo on my lower back. Silence. I thought, *Is she finished? That couldn't be the feedback.* She continued on and said, "I thought you'd want to know that your tattoo was visible. I'm sure you wouldn't want our CEO or anyone else around the table to see it."

Again, I was silent. I was using my learned poker face and desperately refraining from letting any emotion show.

After that moment, though, I was no longer on autopilot. It became crystal clear that this was no longer where I wanted to be. I would no longer give up who I was or how I expressed myself (hair length or body art) or spend my time playing games and making other people

12

happy. In those moments in the boardroom I realized how out of alignment I was with what I desired for myself in my career. This company and the entire setup of my career there had worked fine for me for many years and I was happy to do whatever they asked of me, but in that moment, I once again realized "this is no longer okay."

That was the start of my next reinvention—another huge one at that. I was about to let go of the only status quo I'd ever known in my professional life: working as an employee in a large organization and doing exactly what they requested and required.

Again, the questions flooded my mind: *Who am I without this job or huge company attached to my identity? What am I going to do if I no longer work here? And **what will other people think** if I give up this high-level, high-paying career with a company where I've spent almost eleven years?* In some respects this was even scarier than leaving my marriage.

WAKING UP

Looking back on both of these experiences, I realize how tolerant I had become of my professional and personal life. I tolerated things I knew were not okay because they really weren't "that bad." My life really wasn't bad. In fact, looking in from the outside, you would have thought I had it pretty damn good. When I started to realize that I wasn't happy or got those internal hints of something being off, I pushed them aside because I believed my life was good.

Why would I want to turn things upside down when I was healthy and safe, in a great job, surrounded by lots of love? When I looked around and compared myself to others, to society, and to the awful things that were reported on the news, I knew I had a really great life. However, it was great as defined by others, not by me. Great to me meant a lot

more than appearing great, it meant feeling great, being excited, feeling alive and not being in neutral.

Getting out of neutral meant making some big changes and doing things that felt uncomfortable and scary. It meant letting go of the status quo and reinventing myself with essentially no blueprint. Of course, many others had been in similar situations: single again at thirty-six, leaving my corporate job behind . . . and I could certainly use their blueprints. However, I believed (and still believe) that reinventing yourself and re-creating your life is about doing it on your own terms. The status quo is often so much about what others think and what society says is "acceptable." That was no longer what I wanted my life to be about.

What does "tolerating" really feel like and look like? I'm sure it takes many forms, so my form may look different from others. In my past, I didn't actually realize I had become tolerant of a lifestyle that was not what I wanted, but looking back, it is so clear.

Oprah said something that, in retrospect, speaks vividly to what was occurring in my life while I was in my toleration phase:

> *The Universe speaks to us, always, first in whispers. And a whisper in your life usually feels like "hmm, that's odd." Or, "hmm, that doesn't make any sense." Or, "hmm, is that right?" It's that subtle. And if you don't pay attention to the whisper, it gets louder and louder and louder. I say it's like getting thumped upside the head. If you don't pay attention to that, it's like getting a brick upside your head. You don't pay attention to that—the brick wall falls down. That is the pattern that I see in my life and so many other people's lives. And so, I ask people, "What are the whispers? What's whispering to you now?"*

There were many whispers that I didn't pay attention to. Things would happen in my marriage that would stop me dead in my tracks and I'd literally hear myself saying, "Did that just happen?" or "This cannot be happening. It's not right."

In fact, my whispers were not even of the quiet type. They weren't of the "Hmmm, is that right?" variety. They were more direct, a clear knowing that "This isn't right." Yet I didn't pay attention. I ignored them all, repeatedly, despite how loud they became. I ran away from the knowledge of what was wrong for me.

I spent exorbitant amounts of time at work, traveling, and focusing my energy on my career. I enjoyed being away from my home. If that isn't a loud whisper, what is? I continued to ignore the signs. I was going through the motions, not stopping long enough to pay attention to the many messages around me.

In many respects, I felt numb. Nothing really excited me and there was much more about my married life that I dreaded than looked forward to. Still, I kept moving forward because I had made a commitment and was going to stick to it.

The whispers, screams, and thumps upside the head didn't do it for me, and eventually the brick wall did fall down, but it didn't fall in the way you might imagine. It was an internal crumbling for me. It was the realization that I had spent many years tolerating a life that was not okay with me. My brick wall crumbling was the very noisy breaking of my heart.

That's what developing a tolerance for my personal life looked like—it was actually quite subtle and more like a slow burnout of any excitement or enthusiasm. My career burnout was similar. There were whispers, dealing with politics and wondering who might stab me in

my tattooed back to make themselves look good to the senior vice president of human resources.

The whispers said, "This is an insane way to live every day." I ignored them for a couple of years. I was living by someone else's rules—the rules of my parents (whom I love dearly) and society. Their rules said having a corporate job was the safest, most secure way to have a great career and a great life. Their rules said I needed to follow instructions, say yes when I was asked and do what I was told.

The whispers were telling me that there are other rules to play by—my own. At the time, I didn't pay attention. I forged on believing playing by everyone else's rules was doing the right thing. (Ultimately I believe everything I did in each moment was the right thing because I needed to get to the place where I was ready to make the decision to change.)

Then there were the thumps over the head. I spent the better part of one whole year sick and often not even wanting to get out of bed in the morning. There were occasional days when I had the feeling of dread when I woke up, but mostly there was just no feeling at all. Just numbness. Tolerance. Autopilot. Fortunately I paid enough attention and I made the decision to leave before the brick wall came tumbling down around me.

I believe that going through big life changes and events enables us to continue to develop a "keener sense of self" (as my co-author Julie calls it). It doesn't take too many brick walls to crumble around you before you begin to pay attention to the whispers. It is in that listening to yourself and getting to know, hear, and understand yourself that you grow in your ability to know exactly when it's time to make a change. I believe we all know exactly what we need to do when we need to do it. We just don't trust ourselves enough or pay close enough attention to believe it.

If you think you may be sensing some whispers or knocks upside the head but don't know what to do, don't do anything. I spent years not knowing what to do and did nothing. I don't recommend waiting that long, but I recommend waiting until you know what to do. You *will* know, I assure you, just as I and countless others in similar situations knew. When the time is right, you will know and you will do exactly what is best for you.

So why do we go along feeling okay and happy with life and then… don't? Worse, we realize we've been tolerating "not being okay." I think it's a normal part of evolving through life. We are supposed to become "not okay" with the way things are so we can find new things that continue to expand our lives and the lives of those around us.

Do I think it means you *need* to go through divorces or major career changes? No. I think it means you need to pay attention to what needs attention in your life. Reinventions come in all shapes and sizes. Stay-at-home moms are looking to re-create their lives after their kids are in school fulltime; others may undergo health, body and fitness transformations; some re-create their lives to have a family . . . and when their children are grown . . . and again after losing a loved one. . . .

It's all about being aware of the signs that tell you something is not okay or you're tolerating things in your life that are not working for you anymore. Once you become aware of these things, then you can take steps to begin your own transformation. You can begin to let go of the status quo that no longer works for you.

Once I began my transformation I had an instant feeling of liberation, like letting out a huge exhale. You know the saying "The truth will set you free"? Well, I felt free. I finally admitted something I had known intuitively for a while, and by admitting it, I freed myself from the constraints of having to live out of alignment with who I truly was. I was no longer the "play by the corporate rules" or the "stay in a miserable marriage" type of person, and that was OKAY. Admitting it made it okay. The sky didn't fall and my life pretty much stayed intact, for that moment and many moments afterwards. Admitting it caused an internal shift, which would enable the external shifts that needed to happen in the following months and years.

So despite the fact that nothing "happened" immediately, there was no avoiding that things would need to happen. Once the internal shift occurred, my discontent with the external environment was exacerbated. Living with the external world as it was after I'd had my internal realization and shift was nearly impossible. It was living a lie. Knowing I couldn't live a lie for very long and that I would need to make the external shifts required for me to live my truth were soon followed by the thought, *What the fuck do I do now?*

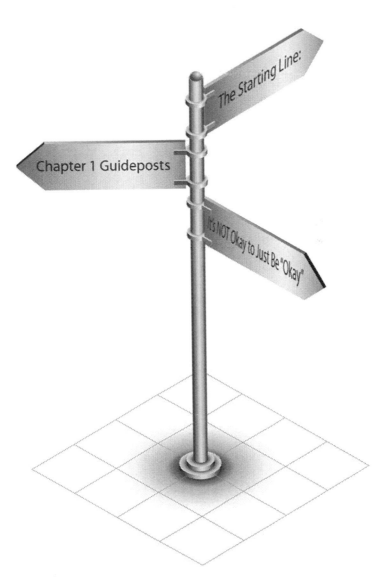

IT'S *NOT* OKAY TO JUST BE "OKAY"

Spend some time getting to know yourself by taking inventory and answering these questions. You don't have to do it all at once, but it is important to answer as many as possible.

What are you tolerating?

In your personal life:

- Spouse/partner
- Children
- Parents
- Friends

In your professional life:

- Career
- Job requirements you aren't good at or don't enjoy
- Co-workers
- Pay
- Professional colleagues
- Networking

What emotions are you feeling?

- Do you ever feel numb, going through the motions? When?
- What is your primary emotion when you think about work or your career?
- When I first wake up in the morning to go to work I feel _____
- Are you passionate about your job? Is it your purpose?
- What's your first and primary emotion about your home life?

When was the last time you got in touch with yourself in thought, prayer, meditation, sitting quietly, walking or hiking alone or dancing (even in your living room)? When was the last time you immersed yourself in an activity you love, such as painting, writing, running or just playing?

Sometimes when people are wondering what their purpose is, they reflect on what they enjoyed as a child. Make a list of things you have enjoyed doing—recreational activities, play, building something, cooking or creative work.

Have you heard the whispers? What are they saying?

Evaluate and be aware, BUT:
- Don't do anything until you know what to do.
- Pay attention to the whispers.
- Trust that you will know what to do when it's time.

Ask yourself:
- What is my definition of failure?
- How do I define success?
- Which would I regret more: trying and not succeeding or not trying at all?
- How do I measure my self-confidence?
- What three things will I do differently in the next month to increase my self-confidence?
- Who is blocking me from increasing my self-confidence?
- Do I want to live this way for the rest of my life?
- If I had two years left to live, would I continue to live this way?

Pay attention to whether your answers are inner-directed (measuring yourself by your own thoughts, feelings or beliefs) or outer-directed (based on what other people think, do, say or believe about you).

CHAPTER 2: SHIFTING GEARS: NEUTRAL TO DRIVE

Once you realize you want your life to be different, there is no turning back. You are now on the path and it is important to take control of the direction you're heading and the life you're creating. You do this by shifting gears, by getting out of neutral and into drive. You are no longer a passenger along for the ride of someone else's life; you are the driver and director of the ride of your life. It's time to take action and make decisions that are aligned with where you want your life to be. The first step is terrifying and empowering and the most difficult to take, but well worth the risk. It's time to let go of what no longer works and actively step into a new way of being—shift gears and proceed forward. There really is no turning back.

—Julie & Andria

Andria's Story

This is your world. Shape it or someone else will.

Finding Me Again

On another Saturday afternoon, I was lying in bed in my new townhouse in New Jersey. It was late March of 2007 and I had left my marriage and my home behind in Pennsylvania. Though closer to my latest job assignment, being in New Jersey didn't excite me. The only saving grace was my proximity to the river, so not only could I run along the river every day, but I could also see the Philadelphia skyline in the distance. Those were about the only two good things I could find in my life during that time.

Did I mention that it was about 3:00 p.m. and I was still in bed, in my pajamas? I might have been hung over, since I had spent most of my free time the prior three months hanging out with people who were several years younger, and drank a lot more than I could. But, if I recall correctly, I wasn't *that* hung over.

My phone rang. It was Smith. I told her I was still in bed. She said, "Just like you were last Saturday, and the Saturday before that. It's beautiful outside, Andria. Get up and go outside."

I had no idea what the weather was like because my room-darkening blinds were doing a fantastic job concealing any hint of daylight.

"By the way," she said, "I'm coming to visit you next weekend to celebrate your birthday." All I could think was, *UGH. MY THIRTY-SEVENTH BIRTHDAY!* When I started to cry, Smith asked me why.

Was she serious? Why wouldn't I be crying and in bed in the middle of a Saturday afternoon at the end of March? I was turning thirty-seven, I was going through *another* divorce and, other than my career, I had no life. Who in their right mind would *not* be crying?

Yep, that was the start of my redesigning my personal life. It wasn't pretty. In fact, I spent a lot of time not knowing what to do, and doing nothing. To me, nothing meant spending weekends lying in bed in my pajamas wallowing in self-pity. It was such an odd time. Looking back, I barely recognize myself.

Three months prior, on Christmas Day, I stood in Debra's foyer (crying, I'm sure, since it was my first Christmas without my husband) and I remember her looking at me with her beautiful brown eyes saying, "One year from now things will look drastically different. Just wait. One year and it will be so much better."

Three months after that, things definitely weren't getting better. In fact, I seemed to be headed in the wrong direction. That is, until my birthday.

As she promised, Smith showed up and dragged me out of the house to celebrate. She was, once again, the voice that got through to me, just as she had the year before with her advice about my marriage. She reminded me that I was a person who could do anything I put my mind to, and recalled many examples of this since the day we met in college almost twenty years earlier.

In addition to her words of wisdom, her gift to me that year was an iPod shuffle including the audio version of the movie *The Secret*. She told me to listen to the audio repeatedly and take action. She reminded me that I was in control of my own destiny, that I was by nature action-oriented and it was time for me to kick it into gear. No more neutral.

25

I saw that I had this blank slate in front of me, and, along with it, this amazing opportunity to create my personal life any way I wanted. As exciting as this seemed, it also seemed daunting. Create my personal life any way I wanted? What did that mean? How could I do that? Who on earth was I outside of my marriage?

And so started the discovery phase of re-creating myself.

We all know who we are, right? Name, gender, and all those titles we acquire: mother, sister, daughter, wife, friend, aunt, homeroom mom, vice president of this, director of that, etc. Despite the fact that I was a sister, daughter, aunt, friend, and human resources leader in a large company, when I lost the title of "wife," I lost a huge piece of myself. Being someone's wife meant I had responsibilities, and I knew what they were. In addition I was a stepmom, and that came with responsibilities, too. I never questioned what I was doing on the weekends or holidays. It was a given. I would be wherever my husband needed to be for his kids. That was the way my life rolled.

Despite the fact that I was unhappy living like that, it was very familiar to me. I knew what was expected. I played by the rules. It worked. I was comfortable because I knew what to expect. When those roles of wife and stepmother were no longer mine, I had to redefine who Andria was.

After my birthday celebration, I realized I had forgotten what I liked to do. I had spent so many years doing whatever my husband wanted and whatever he needed to do to be a good dad to his kids, that I completely lost my sense of self beyond my work/career identity. Now it was time to take action and re-create what it meant to be Andria, the single thirty-seven-year-old woman.

I wasn't sure where to start other than by trying to remember what brought me joy. What did I really enjoy doing in my free time? I had a very demanding job that required a lot of travel so my free time was limited; I became diligent about treating it as sacred "Andria" time. I remember having a free weekend evening shortly after this discovery phase began, and I started to get a bit panicky because I didn't know what to do with myself.

So I asked myself what I had wanted to do over past several years that I hadn't been able to. The answer was so simple and came to me instantaneously: "Go to the bookstore." The bookstore, where I used to spend hours as a child, surrounded by things I love: books. And so I got lost in the many aisles of Borders Books in Moorestown, N.J., and sipped coffee in the café. Thus began my journey of discovering and remembering what it was that Andria liked to do for Andria only.

I had no idea what would be next or what I would want to do next, but during this time some things became clear. I knew I wanted to live closer to Debra and her family in the Washington, D.C., area, and I knew I did not want to get involved in another serious relationship until I had myself figured out. This would mean I knew who I was, an independent woman, and I knew what I wanted from my life, so that any relationship with another man would be an enhancement to what I had already created on my own. I had no clue how to get there but I had a very clear vision of what "there" looked like. The more I grew personally, the clearer this vision became.

How did I grow? I kept asking myself what I wanted to do and reminding myself that there was no one else but me who needed to want it. This was big for me because, like many women, I had spent years ignoring what I wanted to do and what I felt instead doing things that pleased others.

What did I do? I trained for and ran a half marathon, I went to Las Vegas with my friends, I went to the beach with my family, and I jumped at an opportunity to interview for a promotion with my company located in Washington, D.C. Although these may not seem like big things, they were huge to me because they were things I never would have done while I was married.

The more I did things for me, the easier it became. All around me I began to see the meaning of what Smith had told me on my birthday: that I was creating my life the way I wanted it to be. Because I spent most of my adult life *reacting* to things that went on around me, I had given up my power to actually *create* my life.

During my time in New Jersey, I learned how to be an active life participant who created the results I wanted—as opposed to waiting and hoping or just accepting whatever happened. I wanted my life to be drastically different than the prior ten years had been. To do that, I needed to take drastically different actions.

Being an active participant in your life means you are in the driver's seat and not simply along for the ride. It means you are not reacting to your life but actively taking steps towards what you want to happen. Although I've always been a very action-oriented person, I had allowed myself to take a backseat in my personal life; I wanted to keep the peace and be a good wife and stepmother, and I believed that meant I needed to do whatever my husband needed and wanted for his children.

That all changed after I got divorced and began to re-create my personal life and myself. The more decisions I made that were solely based on what was best for me, the more I learned what "best for me" meant. This, in and of itself, was drastically different from what I had been doing for ten years, and it produced drastically different results.

Dating? You've Got to be Kidding! How I Found the Love of My Life

While walking through the Philadelphia airport to catch a flight to Pittsburgh, I ran into Jackie, one of my dearest colleagues and friends, who was headed to Pittsburgh for the same meeting. We didn't know we'd be on the same flight and ended up sitting next to each other. She, too, was in the process of a divorce, so we began talking. She asked me if I was dating. I told her I had dated a little, but wasn't really interested in being in a relationship. I was having a wonderful time being single and re-creating what it meant to be Andria, not Andria as part of a couple.

She told me she thought I should start dating because I am such a wonderful person, have so much to give, etc. I laughed and asked her if she was dating. She said she was on Match.com. I laughed again, not at her but because that was the furthest thing from my mind. She told me that I should try Match and I said, "No way. I do *not* want to get *married* again." She told me that I could create my profile any way I wanted and if I was just interested in casual relationships, I could say that. I tried to ignore her but she didn't let up.

On our return flight, we sat next to each other again and she continued to press me about Match.com. Just to shut her up, I told her I'd think about it and she said, "No you won't. You won't do it."

Was that a challenge? I pondered the conversation for about thirty minutes while Jackie read her book. *Do I want to do this? Maybe it would be fun to meet some new people and go out on a few non-committal dates.*

Internet dating was nothing I'd ever considered. But it *was* drastically different from anything I'd ever done or thought about before.

After some silence, I interrupted Jackie's reading and said, "What do you mean I won't do it?" She said, "I just don't think you will."

And, with that, I accepted the challenge and told her, "I'm doing it."

I got home, set up my profile, and one month later had my first Match.com date with Blue Eyed Fun, aka Matt. Five years later, Matt and I are still together. We own a home and are the very proud parents of four rescue animals.

That is what active, conscious, thoughtful life participation gets you. That is what doing things differently and getting different results means. Had I not taken a chance doing something drastically different like Internet dating, based on a random encounter and a divine conversation, I never would have met Matt, who truly is my perfect match.

Being an active participant in my life also meant a lot of dedicated thought about what constituted a joyful personal life. I spent many hours journaling what I wanted my life to feel like, the types of friends I wanted to surround myself with, the types of fun activities and adventures I wanted to participate in and the type of life partner with whom I could share all those things. Not only did I journal about it but I created vision boards with words and images of the things I wanted to create in my life. I spent so much time on this that by the time I met Matt, much of what I had been seeking in terms of friends and personal satisfaction already existed in my life. Meeting him was the piece of the puzzle that had been missing and he fit into my life so perfectly. Because I had been so actively focusing on what I wanted to continue to enrich the happiness in my life, it was impossible not to recognize it when it showed up as Matt.

When he showed up, he represented that enhancement I was seeking. By the time I met him my personal life was full and complete, based on the things I decided I needed to complete my life without including a partner. He was the icing on the cake that already tasted pretty good without icing. He made my life better because of who he was, not because I was seeking someone to complete my life. I knew completing my life was *my* responsibility.

Being a fully independent, successful man with a complete life of his own, Matt was not seeking someone to complete him, either. He was seeking a relationship and a partner to be the icing on his cake. It became this perfect mix of us sharing our full lives with each other.

After spending time rediscovering who I was outside of my marriage, being in a new relationship meant I would not and could not compromise what I needed to keep my personal life fulfilled. Matt has never asked me to compromise what I need to do to stay connected to what's important to me, whether it includes him or not. I also do the same for him, knowing that if we both are happy in our independent lives and interests, our life together is that much better.

Making the decision to do something different and sign up for Match.com is, to this day, one of the best decisions I ever made.

Re-creating myself professionally included the same active participation as in my personal life; however, it was a different type of journey. I had always been proactive in my professional life but was about to embark on a huge change and make something happen that I had never done before. This meant being proactive in a different way.

Sometime during 2008, I was in my large, beautiful, executive office on the phone with Debra, coughing incessantly from an upper respiratory infection. "Why don't you just quit?" she asked.

What? I thought I misheard because I had been coughing so loudly. "Quit," she said. "You hate it there; you've hated it there for a while. Everyone stabs everyone in the back—it's insane. Just quit and do something else or go work for someone else. It's ridiculous to stay in such a stressful and miserable environment."

My retort was, "I can't JUST QUIT."

She said, "Why not? You don't have any kids to feed. It's just you. Quit for heaven's sake."

"And who's gonna pay my mortgage and my bills?" I asked. "It's not like I'm you, a stay-at-home mom with a husband to support me and pay my bills. So, no, I cannot JUST QUIT." And with that, we hung up. She had hit a nerve.

Her voice and words stayed in my head for months. The unhappier I got at work, the louder I heard them. I started to see "behind the curtain" at work, tired of playing their games and working seventy hours a week without seeming to get anything done. I became more and more out of alignment with my true self. I knew deep down that I had to go, and finally made my decision after the unforgettable tattoo comment from my boss.

Once I made that decision, things got even harder because I knew I was going to leave but I didn't know how to be in that environment and not give 1000 percent. So there I was, running at full speed without my heart in the race. It was exhausting. But as the action-oriented activator in my career, it was easy for me to put my exit strategy together. First I considered going to work for another company. After a brief search into the possibilities, it looked like a lot more of the same.

Matt and Smith both planted the bug in my ear to start my own business. They felt I was self-motivated enough to easily make a success of any company I started. I loved them for their faith in me but the idea of running my own company was not exactly on my radar—truthfully, it petrified me.

Starting my own business was a foreign concept to a girl who'd grown up playing by the rules: Go to school, get as much education as possible, and then get a really good job in a really good stable company. Period.

These were the rules set by influential people as I grew up and that I truly believed were requirements for a successful career. In fact, my dad's voice was always the loudest in my head. He had spent thirty-plus years successfully climbing the corporate ladder at a large corporation, and strongly encouraged me to take the same path.

Now I was questioning the rules. I realized that they were set by very smart and loving people, but they were rules that worked for *them*. Could I seek my own set of rules and redefine what was best for me in my professional life? The "job at a really good stable company" was no longer something I wanted. Yet letting go of rules I had hung on to so tightly for most of my life and letting go of what was familiar was scary. I wasn't sure how to get over my fear but knew I needed to if I was to live life on my own terms.

A couple of months after that conversation with Debra, Matt and I were on vacation with Smith and her husband, Ross. Sitting at dinner one night after drinks, I was chatting with Ross, who owns his own business. He, too, started telling me that I should start my own company.

"Andria," he said. "You think you're secure working for that big company but they can turn around tomorrow and close up shop or eliminate your job. That's not security. Security is working for yourself because you are relying on yourself and you will never let yourself down. That's being secure about your income and your success."

And there it was—another divine message from the Universe. *So be it,* I thought at that table. *I will start my own business.*

I texted Debra to tell her I was quitting my job. We had a text celebration and of course she wanted to know WHEN?! It would be another eight months before things all came together so I could leave the corporate world and launch my company, C3 Coaching & Consulting. Despite the fact that I had no children and only myself and my animals to feed, it was not easy to forego the security of a regular paycheck. I didn't have anyone to rely on but me, and although I was very confident in my abilities to succeed at anything I put my mind to, I had no idea how to run a business and no one to fall back on if it didn't work.

I pushed myself through the doubts and created my action plan for C3. This plan included what I needed financially and what needed to get done when. I did a lot of research and worked with a coach during my last six months in the corporate world. I put my business plan together and took all the necessary steps to make sure that I was ready to hit the ground running when I left my job.

One of my biggest obstacles was getting past the chatter in my head that asked, *What will everyone think?* I had to resolve that before I could even contemplate sharing my decision with anyone other than my very trusted inner circle. I knew I was doing the right thing, but worried that what other people might say would make me second-guess my decision.

Most people would think I was crazy to give up all I had. I was on a fast-moving career path climbing the ladder in a large, stable, well-run and well-known company. I had a pension, great benefits and tons of potential. So I had to remind myself of what my coach said: "What others think about me is none of my business."

I have no idea what people truly thought when I shared my news with them. I consciously decided that it was my decision and mine alone. Nothing was going to change my mind, even the naysayers and all the crazy news about the recession. I had begun my journey but the real reinvention didn't start until the day after I left the corporate world and that image behind.

Early in 2010 I started my business, feeling like a fish out of water. I was so used to being a leader with a big company name behind me. Again, I had to figure out who I was. Yes, now I was the owner of C3, but as a brand-new startup, I wasn't even sure what C3's identity was. In fact, we are now into our third year in business and C3's identity continues to evolve. I think it will be an ongoing process.

As with my personal life, re-creating myself as a business owner meant I had to be in the driver's seat at all times. Reacting to what was going on around me would have been a recipe for failure. I had to drive my business forward and create it as I wanted it to be. I felt much more time pressure when I started C3 than when I was redesigning my personal life—I needed clients so I could make money.

I charted my course by imagining being a successful business owner. How did successful business owners act? What did they do? I followed suit, but only to a certain extent. I obviously didn't want to do anything that wasn't in the best interest of C3's growth and my own sanity. And, as I mentioned before, the whole idea of re-creating myself professionally and creating C3 was to do it *on my terms*. It was about what was going to work best for this business and me.

I took steps based on what I knew and learned from others and what felt right to me. I never stopped moving forward. Yes, there were plenty of setbacks, but I didn't look at them as mistakes. I looked at them as figuring out how to do things better. I refrained from asking for too much advice from my loved ones because they all had different opinions and I wanted to remain true to the direction I believed to be best for my company.

Every day, taking steps to move along my path was crucial to becoming an active participant in creating not only a successful business, but in re-creating myself as a successful business owner. We touch upon many of the mistakes, lessons, and steps in future chapters, but this element of being an active participant in my life was crucial to re-creating myself.

That concept of not doing anything when you don't know what to do can actually be a very active approach. Paying attention to your intuition and the whispers until you are propelled into movement *is* being in the driver's seat. Active participation is being aware of when you are and aren't ready to do things and doing only those things that are in your best interest. Knowing not to move because you don't know where to go *is* active participation. It is precisely when you don't know what to do, but are led by someone else's desires or rules that don't resonate with you, that you give up your participation in your life.

I don't believe you can re-create yourself or redesign your life if you are a passenger. The saying "This is your world. Shape it or someone else will" describes this perfectly. Unless you are in the driver's seat, someone else will be leading the way. If you want to redesign your life or re-create some aspect of who you are, you must drive that re-creation; otherwise it will not be on your own terms, but on the terms of whom you've allowed into the driver's seat. This means letting go of what others want you to be and creating your life as you want it to be.

This doesn't mean you ignore your loved ones or your responsibilities to them, it means you incorporate those responsibilities into your reinvention in a way that best fits the person you want to be. As Oprah puts it: *"You define your own life. Don't let other people write your script."*

Julie's Story

If you don't know where you are going any road will get you there.
— Lewis Carroll, author of *Alice in Wonderland*

WE MAKE PLANS, GOD LAUGHS

In order to redefine the life you want you must truly understand what you are seeking.

*What is the ultimate goal you have for your life? If you can't describe your ultimate goal, can you define your short-term objectives? Have you even given yourself the opportunity to contemplate what you **want** instead of simply doing what is required of you?*

Once you can clearly articulate the goals for your journey, you can begin to make the necessary modifications to your life so you can move toward your goals. Something as simple as writing down a goal can be all the motivation you need to begin to change your life.

Something sparked your interest in reading this book. What specific actions led you here to this very moment? Was it a single event or a series of seemingly unrelated situations? Harness the power of the subtle message life sent you to start or continue your journey of redefining your life.

Consider your present life when answering the following questions:

- What do you love about your life?
- What would you change in a heartbeat if given the chance?
- What would you like to start doing?
- What do you wish you could stop doing?
- What are the top three things you need to continue doing to ensure you are satisfied?

Something spoke to you to revisit your life journey. There is an impetus somewhere in your life to make a change. You are not alone. Many, many women before you have jumped from the passenger seat to the driver's seat in their own lives and created the fulfillment they desired.

My journey began when I became an active participant in my life. The pivotal moment occurred when I decided not to simply accept the mediocrity of my job and sought to intentionally find my ideal next role. Being an active participant in my life was the single biggest change agent in my journey and continues to be critical to my successful reinvention journey. Without it, I could not advance. I was running in place, trying over and over again to move along in my journey, yet not making any forward progress.

Until you move from neutral to drive, you continually set yourself up for failure. We all know people who seem to be constantly subjected to the cruelty of life—the people who always have bad things happen to them time and time again. How much of that is chance? Could it be they are *passengers* in their own lives? We can't control everything in life, however *we can control how we react to things*. And we can anticipate and respond much more easily from the driver's seat than the passenger seat.

Remember the perfect job I finally landed? The amazing, ideal match to my list of must-haves? The job I found when I left my safe, comfortable position? The gold ring I finally received?

Well, it didn't turn out as I expected. The Universe had bigger plans for me than I could ever have dreamt. I'd been with my current employer for several years, and creating a smooth transition leading up to my departure was my priority. My clients were extremely supportive of my career advancement. While they wished opportunities for me were available within the company, they fully appreciated my situation and respected my desire to climb the corporate ladder. They gave me wonderful compliments about my contributions and wished me well in my future endeavors.

After a three-week transition, my last day arrived. In order to make the most of the transition, my last day was the first day of the month. Ever the planner, I wanted to mitigate any risk during the transition from one job to another. If my last day with my company was on the first of the month, I'd be eligible for healthcare for the entire month. With mixed emotions, I exited the building, closing one chapter and about to open another.

The new company wanted me to start right away. I arranged to take two days off before starting my new gig to get a few things in order. On the first morning of my staycation, my phone rang. The caller ID spelled out my new company. Maybe they were changing the time I was supposed to show up for orientation? I picked up the phone and heard the voice of my new supervisor on the other end. Did I have a few minutes to talk? Sure thing! He explained that, unfortunately, the funding for my position had been eliminated. I would no longer be starting on Monday.

When I was least prepared for it, life threw me a big curveball. This was **not** what I planned! I panicked. I couldn't catch my breath and found myself struggling to stand up. It felt like I was having a panic attack. Was this some kind of joke?

I asked him to repeat what he told me. He did and it stung just as much the second time. How could this be happening to me? I did everything right! I crossed the t's and dotted the i's. Things like this don't happen to me. I'm smart and capable. I've been working since I was twelve years old.

But suddenly I was unemployed.

I hung up the phone. Tears sprung to my eyes. I melted into a ball on my kitchen floor. Could this really be happening to me? What would I tell my husband? He was so proud of me for getting this amazing job and now I was unemployed. Did I mention it was the worst job market in decades? How would I find another job?

Once I was able to actually digest the phone call I made a conscious choice: I assumed the drivers' seat. I took control of the situation and that made all the difference in how I was able to redefine my life.

After several conversations with Greg, the obvious choice I'd been reluctant to make became crystal clear: I would start my own company. One week after the most devastating news in my career, I embarked on a journey that turned out to be the best professional decision I ever made. I sat in the driver's seat and took control of the steering wheel.

It wasn't easy rebounding from the loss of my ideal position to start a business, however each and every day I set goals for myself that kept me moving forward. One day it was simply getting out of bed and attending a networking event. Defining how I was going to use my time each day became increasingly important. I found when I put one foot in front of the other and took forward motion, I gained confidence. To say my professional confidence was damaged by the loss of the ideal job I'd worked for fifteen years to attain is an understatement.

When I got my first client, my confidence began to rebound as well. When my second client hired me, I found myself walking taller. Within three months of starting the business I had secured a handful of terrific clients and found I was busier than ever.

CHILDLESS AND CHOOSING

I've moved from neutral to drive in my personal life as well as my professional life. The decision to have children wasn't an easy one for me. Some women grow up knowing they will be mothers. Most of my friends were moms by the time they were thirty years old. I have loved children for as long as I can remember. Babysitting was an instrumental part of my life from the age of twelve. I've had the privilege of being involved in the lives of several amazing children. However, becoming a mother myself was one thing I knew I could never *un*do—that terrified me beyond measure.

After I graduated from college and started working, here's where my thinking was: I knew I wanted to have a career and find success in the business world. I also knew I wanted to find a spouse who shared my values and build a life together. Travel was high on my priority list. Seeing new places, meeting new people and possibly living in Europe were all on my bucket list.

Where did kids fit into my ideal life? After much introspection I wasn't confident I was cut out for motherhood. I wasn't sure I was capable of the sacrifices it took to be a mom. How would my career fit into motherhood? And where was that maternal instinct, anyway? Why wasn't my biological clock ticking like it was for all my friends?

So I postponed making a decision until I was confident in my choice. Greg and I had many conversations about children before we got married. We were on the same page: We wanted to build a life together and that life might or might not include children. We agreed we both needed to be comfortable with having a child in order to take the leap into parenthood.

For the first five years of marriage we were happily child-free. In fact, Greg and I communicated a unified message: "child-free by choice." This tended to shut down the ever-present lingering question friends and family members had: "When are you going to have children?" Since we honestly didn't know when, or if, we would have children, we simply decided to say, "Never." Our families and friends accepted our decision but I'm not sure they really ever understood. Many suggested we would change our minds, and perhaps we would, but at that point in our lives we were confidently living *sans* kids and weren't afraid to own our choice, publicly or privately.

Our decision not to have children made some people very uncomfortable. Why weren't we following the traditional path: college, career, marriage, house, dog, and kids? I experienced numerous situations in which people clearly didn't understand. I was quick to point out that we didn't want kids at this point. Yes, we were happily married. No, there was no reason to believe we couldn't have kids. We simply elected not to have them. Despite my ability to own our decision not to have children, without fail people would respond with "Oh," as their eyes exhibited pity. Parents simply couldn't imagine a life without children.

One night, Greg and I had dinner with several other couples, all of whom had children. We only knew one couple well, so it was an opportunity to get to know their friends. The conversation turned to the same old topic: our lack of kids. It wasn't uncommon for us to be the only people who didn't; we'd come to expect addressing the "whys." We would jokingly speculate who would be the brave one to ask us the question. At this dinner, I won that bet. I knew the loud New Yorker would be the one who asked the inappropriate question.

However, his delivery threw me off: "So what do you do with your time? I can't imagine being single. What is that like?"

This was a new one for us. I tend to be direct and have a dry sense of humor so I responded, "Well, I'm not single. Greg and I have been married for seven years and I'm pretty sure he wouldn't be happy if I acted like a single chick. And the answer to your question is we do whatever the HELL we want whenever the HELL we want to for as long as we want to. It is actually quite liberating. Oh, and we have lots of sex." I managed to shut him up quickly and he changed the topic. Fortunately it was near the end of the meal, so we made a graceful exit.

I was angry and frustrated during the drive home. What right did this virtual stranger have to interrogate me about my life choices?

Then I paused. Why was *I* so fired up by the question? I was asked why we didn't have kids frequently but this time it was different. Why wasn't I confident in our decision? Was I changing my mind? More infuriating to me was that Greg was not subjected to these questions. Why was it an expectation that family planning details were handled out of the "First Lady's Office"?

I knew as long as we were comfortable with our decision it didn't really matter what anyone else thought. It seems so obvious, doesn't it? As long as you are confident with your choices, who cares what anyone else thinks? However, with such a personal and permanent outcome, it took me a long time to be confident in my decision to remain child-free by choice.

Part of the journey was getting to know myself better and growing closer to Greg. For me the decision to have a child was the one decision I would never be able to reverse. Yes, I went into my marriage not thinking we would get divorced, but let's be honest, 50 percent of marriages end in divorce. I knew if things didn't work out, for whatever reason, I would be okay. I am a survivor. Being a mom took this to a whole new level. I knew I wanted to be extremely comfortable with my decision when, and if, I decided to have a child.

A few months after that dinner, I had my annual exam. I was in my early thirties. As if the anticipation of this appointment wasn't bad enough, I began to dread the appointment because I was getting older, which meant my eggs were also aging. I couldn't avoid reading articles or hearing news broadcasts detailing the challenges of women having children later in life.

After the general pleasantries of the appointment were out of the way, the lovely nurse cautiously asked if we intended to have children. I answered, "Not at this time," to which she gently pointed out I was getting older and increased maternal age can be linked to higher risks for the baby.

While I appreciated her looking out for me and the health of my yet-to-be-conceived child, I was rocked by the conversation. What had changed in me? Why did hearing things I already knew have such a tremendous impact? Why wasn't my husband forced to hear this conversation?

I decided I needed more time for introspection and honest conversations with myself.

So we planned the year of "child-free by choice." We embraced living without children to the extreme. We made a list of things we wanted to do without kids and began to cross things off our list. We traveled extensively. We grew closer as a couple. We relished time with our friends. We embraced "OPC" (other people's children) and loved returning them to their parents at the conclusion of our play dates.

Then, after a year, we evaluated how we felt. Greg and I were able to communicate effectively throughout this journey. The conversations were not always welcome but certainly necessary. Greg is extremely perceptive. I am eternally grateful to him for making me talk about things even when I say I'm not ready. After our year of self-indulgence, Greg was ready for parenthood. I, however, was still not confident. So the waiting game continued.

Ultimately I decided I was ready. Yes, I was going to be a mother! Finally I was comfortable with the decision. But timing is everything. Just when I was confident in my decision, Greg wasn't sure! Now the timing seemed wrong for him. His career was beginning to take off and he had just landed an incredible new role with a new company. He was traveling a lot and it didn't seem like the right time to start a family. Would we ever be on the same page? How many conversations would end with me in tears? How long could we continue this dance of indecision?

While taking a walk on my thirty-fifth birthday, we both decided it was now or never. After an exhausting process, we were both ready for the next chapter in our lives and mutually agreed it included a child. By continuing to communicate our fears, expectations, hopes and feelings, we went from child-free by choice to officially trying to start a family.

The journey taught me to be confident in my decision and not back down to pressure from anyone. I learned the importance of knowing myself and truly understanding not only what I desire but also the motivations behind it. Reflecting on those three years of transition from child-free by choice to officially wanting to be a mom, it is clear to me I needed to give myself the time, space and energy to fully make and own my decisions.

Indecision was a significant part of my going from no to yes on parenthood. If you are struggling with a decision, don't be afraid to give yourself the time to contemplate the decision. I found this was one decision I couldn't force, despite my best efforts.

I am sure you are faced with equally significant choices as you let go of the status quo in your life. It was unconventional to be in a happy, childless marriage and this caused friction from other people. I became stronger in my decision the more I lived with it. Unfortunately, I didn't have the road map or specific date and time when the decision would officially be made, and that was frustrating. Being a type A person who plans everything, this was part of the journey I simply had to relinquish control over and trust it would happen when it was supposed to happen—a lesson I've learned over and over again since then.

NEUTRAL TO DRIVE

Evaluate Your Feelings

You know that feeling you get when you've made a decision and it feels "right." Something calm and enlivening settles into your gut and begins to propel you forward. The murkiness disappears, the "buts" and "what ifs" fade away into "I _will_ make this happen," "I _will_ see this through," and you become confident in your role as an active participant in your life.

Unfortunately, those times of indecision can last longer than you'd like, moving you back and forth to yes, then to no, and back yet again. You may remain confused and sometimes stuck.

What can you do?

- Take baby steps. Do not move, make decisions, or tell anyone outside your circle what you're working through.
- Do not ask for advice unless you know this person is an unqualified supporter, trusted mentor or coach who can see your blind spots and cheer you on.
- Find a medium though which your deepest thoughts can come out. Write down all of your feelings, where you see yourself in the future, what you want and "THE WHY." What do you think you will receive by having these things, in other words what is the essence of the things you want—happiness, love, joy, connection, security, peace . . . ?
- Whether you are artistic or not, the activity of creating vision boards is powerful. Your subconscious mind deals in images and continues to work with those pictures well after you've pasted them on your board.

- Create an action plan, even if it's only the next baby step, to move in the direction of where you want to be. Every day, take at least one step, however small, toward your goal. Keep a record of your steps and check them off.

- Remember to take one step at a time. If you begin to worry how all the steps will fit into place and when, you may push yourself into overwhelm and freeze again. Each time you take a step changes the probabilities anyway.

- Acknowledge yourself when you make a decision. Making a decision is powerful.

- Make your decisions from the place where you want to be.

- Keep your focus on your end goal and objective. Do not allow yourself to worry about all of the "hows." Make the decision and *know* it will come to pass.

- Stop listening to what other people think you should do or be.

- Be in the driver's seat; take responsibility for everything in your life. What you ignore or blame others for will only come back to haunt you.

- Make up your own rules and stop playing by everyone else's.

Ask Yourself:

- Who do you think are active life participants? Which decisive and bold achievers do you admire? Put them on your vision board.

- How are you an active participant in your own life?

- What can you do tomorrow to take the wheel in some small way?

- What do you want your life to look like? Keep journaling about it and visualizing it in meditation.

CHAPTER 3:
CREATING SPACE

As you proceed along your path of letting go of the status quo, the concept of creating space is essential. Why? Because you need to be able to hear both internal and external messages as you move through your journey. Oftentimes you get so busy you don't slow down enough to pay attention to how you feel or what your internal voice is saying. Creating space and/or quiet time in your life is what allows these important messages to get through, sink in, and help guide you along your path.

At first you may not like what you hear. Keep listening! By allowing yourself space and time to hear the messages, you facilitate change. Creating space is as important as the previous elements of taking action and being in the driver's seat. Creating space helps ensure those actions are in alignment with what you truly desire your life to be. Embrace the silence!

—Julie & Andria

Andria's Story

SLOW DOWN, YOU MOVE TOO FAST

As I began letting go of my status quo in both my personal and professional lives, I realized there were many messages I received along the way that I didn't hear or heed. Today, I know I heard exactly what I needed to hear when I needed to hear it for my journey to unfold perfectly; yet looking back I recognize the many things going on with me internally that prevented those messages from registering.

Prior to my hearing the important messages that drove me to make a change, there were some obvious things occurring, both personally and professionally, which drowned out the signposts. The primary thing was a desire to keep myself excessively busy. While I was married, I never allowed myself to stop long enough to hear anything going on internally, or externally for that matter. I was so busy traveling and doing what was required of me as a wife and a stepmom on the weekends that there was no time to slow down, let alone slow down and _listen_.

From age eight until I was twenty-five, I kept journals. This was cathartic and therapeutic. I loved writing, especially about my experiences and feelings. Journaling was a way to understand why I felt the way I did and create space to understand myself and what I needed. Yet once I hit my mid-twenties, I stopped keeping a journal because I was too busy. Along with running, journaling had always been a wonderful way for me to take time to slow down. Although I continued to run while married, I always felt rushed. I only had a certain amount of time to run before work, and on the weekends my husband was always waiting for me to go somewhere so I'd rush through my runs, which ended up being anything but therapeutic or cathartic.

52

The common theme was that I was rushing through everything and not taking any time to simply slow down and experience not only what was going on around me, but also experience my feelings enough to listen to what they were telling me. I think I kept this pace for so many years because I was afraid to slow down. If I slowed down and paid attention, I would have had to confront some very uncomfortable things. And so, I kept rushing from here to there, ignoring the many whispers and thumps upside the head that were all around me.

Then I was forced to stop and slow down shortly before I decided to end my marriage. I was out running (likely rushing through it) and slipped on black ice. I spent six weeks laid up with a broken ankle. Immediately afterwards, I spent a few days at home, allowing the pain and swelling to subside so I could get myself into a walking boot-cast. I was by myself, with my dogs, not on the computer, unable to keep up with work tasks. It was probably the first time in years I was surrounded by nothing but my dogs and myself. In those few moments of quiet and solitude I remember looking around at my big, beautiful house and chuckling to myself as I had a faraway thought: *What a nice façade you have created, Andria.* Immediately I shook myself into conscious awareness and told myself: *Stop it. It's a beautiful home. You're healthy, aside from this stupid broken ankle, which will heal soon, and you have a good life.*

Despite my trying to rationalize those thoughts I became aware of in the quiet solitude, I couldn't escape the messages that started to come through. They were very clear: *Whose life is this? How did I end up here? I don't want to be here. I am not happy. We are not happy. We are miserable. My dogs deserve to be in a home surrounded by loving energy and not tense, anxious energy.* It was as if these thoughts and feelings were buried deep in my subconscious and just waiting for an opening so they could break through. In that quietness, I unknowingly created space for myself to hear some very crucial messages.

Today I see my broken ankle as the catalyst that allowed me to hear messages about how I was living my life. That break was a divine intervention for me because it forced me to do something I never would have done if it hadn't happened: slow down. And in the slowing down, I had no choice but to become acutely aware of what was going on around me; I had no choice but to acknowledge what I had tried so desperately to ignore for many years.

After I healed enough to get my walking cast, I quickly returned to my routine of rushing through my life and ignoring what was going on for me personally. However, I couldn't change the fact that I had actually slowed down enough to hear some significant messages, and, beyond hearing them, had actually acknowledged their truth. Before that time, I heard messages but never paid attention long enough to acknowledge them. I pushed them back into my subconscious with my rational and practical justifications and moved forward.

The difference at this point was that because I had acknowledged their truth, they were now in the forefront of my mind. I (now) know that is why I was able to hear, loud and clear, what Smith said to me on the phone shortly thereafter: "Do you want to live like this for the rest of your life?"

Had she asked me that question prior to my broken ankle (and for all I was aware, she probably did ask me that question many times), I would have brushed it off and probably told her that it wasn't all that bad. I would have heard her but it would not have registered, nor would I have acknowledged there being any truth to what I was hearing.

Looking back on that time in my life made me realize the importance of creating space to hear and acknowledge important messages. When I say "creating space," I mean slowing down. I mean stopping to pay attention to what is going on around you. I mean recognizing and acknowledging what you are feeling. Today I practice meditation as a wonderful way to slow down and quiet my mind enough to receive important messages.

Back when I was married and in my corporate job, the idea of meditation made me laugh. Quiet my mind? I didn't have time for that! What I love is that despite the fact that I didn't have time to even slow down, let alone meditate, the messages still got through. The Universe found a way to get through to me and ensure that I heard what I needed to hear. It had to happen in the form of an injury. It was as if my body knew that was the only way to get me to slow down enough to pay attention. I had no other choice. I am so grateful that I slipped on that black ice and broke my ankle that day.

Today I know that the Universe is always speaking to us—through our friends, family, phone conversations, songs on the radio and conversations we overhear. The messages are always there. The question is are we listening and what do we hear?

By the time I realized I needed to leave my corporate job, I had already created enough space in my life that those messages were able to reach me more easily than when I was in my marriage. That's not to say I didn't ignore them. I did, repeatedly. I would hear my inner voice telling me that there had to be something better, that I wanted something different, that there must be a different way for me to be a successful career woman; however, I rationalized those thoughts away with my much stronger rationalizations: *This is the right path to take to have a successful career, I am getting paid really good money, there is so much growth opportunity here, and people would think I was crazy if I left.*

Yet the more dissatisfied I became, the louder those messages became—not only internally but also externally. The loudest was when Debra told me to quit. Ultimately it was harder to ignore these messages about my career than with my marriage. Despite how busy I kept myself and how much I tried to push the thoughts and messages aside, there was enough space in my life for them to get through and for me to actually acknowledge them as truth.

People have asked me how I distinguish truthful messages from fear-based messages. For example, how did I know that hearing my inner voice say, *There has to be a better path to take to have a successful career* was truth versus when I heard it ask, *Who are you to launch your own business in the middle of a recession?* The best answer I have is that you just *know*.

I felt so deeply in my gut that there was a better path for me to take and that when I asked myself the "Who are you to do this?" question it felt shallower than it had before. It was the voice of doubt versus the voice of reason. I knew this because of how differently each of those thoughts made me *feel*. I did not want to take action based on fear. I wanted to take action based on what I knew was right for me. Not starting a business would have been fear-based (non)action. Moving forward with my plan was action based on what was best for me. I just knew, and you will, too.

To better distinguish, create the space in your life to ponder these types of questions. If I wasn't sure whether it was my truth or my fear speaking, I would journal about it or go on a long run and clear my mind as much as possible, all the while believing the right answer would come to me. It always did and it always does. You will never be led astray when you trust your instincts. It doesn't mean everything always works out perfectly but it does mean you are making decisions that are best for you at the time. This is what creating space allows you to do: listen to your own instincts and learn to trust them as you move forward.

For some people, creating space in life means spending time in nature, getting a massage, or listening to music that allows them to get clear on what their instincts are telling them. For others, it's meditation. For me, it's meditation, journaling, and running.

Whether you spend time in nature, get a massage, go running or do meditation and journaling to allow yourself that time and space, it's really important that you have boundaries in place that protect this sacred time. After all, you are working through what is necessary to reinvent yourself. As I continue to evolve, time for me to make the right and best decisions is something that must be protected and something I must honor as I do all my other appointments. As women it's so easy to put ourselves last, but when we do that we end up having nothing to give anyone else. Boundaries are really important here.

First are the physical boundaries. Make a regular appointment with yourself, daily, weekly, or whatever works best for you, to take time to nurture yourself. Don't break this appointment. Treat it like you would a business appointment or your child's doctor's appointment. Doing this for yourself may feel uncomfortable at first but the more you do it, the easier it becomes and the more you will recognize how important it is for your well-being. This is how you can hear and acknowledge the important messages that are all around you.

When I was in my second year of business, I was traveling on the train back home from New York where I had been doing some work for a client. During that train ride, I was sitting near two women who were having a conversation. I was half listening to them, but I did overhear one of them say something loud and clear: "If you just designed your own training program, you could then work it into the overall schedule."

For the prior few weeks, I had been contemplating some new services to launch in my business but wasn't quite sure what that meant. It was while I was out on a run, the day after that train ride, that I received the answer to what I had been contemplating for weeks. As I was running (honoring my daily time and space for me), I started to think about what I could launch that would be new and different for my business the next year. And I heard the answer in that woman's voice from the train: "If you just designed your own program . . .". I knew instantly what I was supposed to do: design my own coaching program for my clients.

That is just one example of how powerful creating space and self-nurturing time can be. You will get the answers to your questions, you will know what you need to do to continue to take action towards your goal, and you will be able to acknowledge what feelings you have and what they actually mean. Of course you may try to push some things aside, and that's okay. The point is to create the time and space to allow what you are ready to receive to get through.

Setting boundaries is also about emotional and cognitive boundaries —who and what you allow to impact you emotionally and what thoughts and beliefs you allow to dominate your mind. Will they support your self-nurturing or not?

For example, when I started my business, I had to keep myself away from the news reports of how awful the economy was and how we were not coming out of this recession anytime soon. It would have been so easy for me to watch CNN twenty-four hours a day and clutter my head with all that negativity, but I had to set boundaries to prevent that. I wanted to keep my mind open to the possibilities that were all around me instead of filling it with fear-based news media. If I cluttered my mind with all the negative "what ifs," there would be little space for me to hear the positive, non-fear-based messages that were also all around me. Just like with physical boundaries, I also needed to establish and honor emotional and cognitive boundaries.

Nurturing space is such an important ingredient for reinvention, but you may wonder how to create it for yourself. At first, it was forced upon me by my broken ankle, and that was when I learned how important it was to slow down and pay attention. And then it was simply a choice. After experiencing how crucial this was to hearing essential information and remembering when I used to take this kind of time for myself through journaling and running, I decided that self-nurturing space needed to be a regular part of my life. Always.

But I had to remind myself that my runs were meant to be self-nurturing, not rushed (since rushing had become the habit). I had to schedule journaling time each evening and meditation time each morning. It took a while before these new activities became habits. And even though they are habits today, they still don't happen every day. That's okay. They happen consistently enough.

I've also gotten comments from others about it being "easy" for me to do these things because I don't have children. That is true. I don't have children. I have other responsibilities. I have pets, a boyfriend, a home to take care of and a business to run, but no children. Whether your responsibilities include children or not, you still need to keep making that choice for yourself.

I know when I don't take time for myself and meditation, running, or journaling, I can't hear my internal voice or even make sense of the messages that are being given to me, and I'm not at my best for anyone, including myself. That would be true whether I had children or not.

Even without kids, I still found plenty of excuses to not create space for myself. Again, you get to decide. I hope you decide on self-nurturing time and space, regardless of your responsibilities.

Once you create this amazing open space in your life, what happens? So many things that I think the better question is what do you *do* with all that happens? By virtue of the fact that you are spending time with yourself and taking self-nurturing actions, you will notice things you had not noticed before: ideas, feelings, inspirational thoughts. Ultimately, you get to decide what you want to do with that information. The point is to be aware of all you begin to experience during these moments and then decide on the best action to take for yourself based on where you are right now.

This concept of creating space and self-nurturing time opens you up for all of the possibilities of what you can become. It allows you to contemplate your options and continue to redesign yourself and your life on your terms. Because this time is all about you, it allows you to fully experience being who you are truly seeking to become, if only as an idea at first.

I remember during many of my runs and journaling sessions while living in New Jersey, I contemplated what it would mean for me to get into another relationship by vividly imagining who I would *be* in that new relationship. As I did that, I thought through what felt the best to me about being in a relationship and how it would fit into the life I wanted to create for myself and the person I wanted to be both in and outside of that relationship. It was from this contemplative state that I was able to act on what I knew was best for me.

Similarly, when I began to put my business plan together and consider what my business would look like, how it would operate and what it would be like to be a successful business owner, I was able to create it exactly as I wanted during my quiet moments of self-nurturing contemplation. During these times, I further mulled ideas that came to me and ended up tossing aside many that did not resonate with me. I would not have been able to actively re-create my life as it is today, and continue to evolve in my life, if I had not had time and space for thoughtful contemplation. It is one of the vital aspects of being able to reinvent yourself in such a way that is not only on your own terms, but in true alignment with who you want to be.

Creating space enables you to take inspired and aligned actions as an active participant in your life. Sometimes if we don't take time to be thoughtful, to self-nurture and to truly tap in to our instincts, our actions may not be as fruitful. When we are acting from a place of truly knowing that what we are doing is right for us, the action becomes much more natural. Combining self-nurturing activities that allow you some open space and time with being in the driver's seat of your life can and will continue to support you in re-creating yourself and your life in an increasingly graceful and effortless way.

Julie's Story:

INVESTING IN YOURSELF

Hold on to sixteen as long as you can
Changes come around real soon
Make us women and men
> —*from "Jack and Diane" by John Cougar Mellencamp*

I've been a music-lover all my life. Kristi and I were children of the 1970s and our father loved country and western music, as it was called in those days. I recall being in the back seat of our old, blue Toyota Corolla listening to Dolly Parton, Kenny Rogers and The Carpenters. I still find music motivating, comforting, relaxing and cathartic. Each and every day there is music in my world and it creates the space I need to hear the messages along my life's journey.

When I hear a specific song, it takes me back to a point in time and I can vividly remember the emotions, smells, sights and people who were with me during the making of that memory. John Cougar Mellencamp's "Jack and Diane" will always remind me of the month before my seventeenth birthday. As we cruised with no place to go, a high school friend blared the song in his car. We were footloose and fancy-free. Not a care in the world and unaware of the life-changing events the future would bring. Every time I hear the song I'm almost seventeen and loving the freedom it represents.

I love television and social media. I tweet, I use Facebook, and I've been known to spend entirely too much time on pinning things on Pinterest. As I continued my journey, it became clear to me that when other people are talking I am not provided with the opportunity to listen to the messages life is sending my way. I discovered it is okay to set boundaries even with things you enjoy. I try each and every day to adhere to the self-imposed parameters I've established in certain aspects of my life.

Although sometimes I wish I could just chat on Facebook and lose myself in another marathon of the latest reality show drama, one of the most important lessons I've learned is that I am simply a more fulfilled person when I give myself set boundaries for myself. I find I can always make excuses about why I don't have time to journal or read or even write, however I am ultimately the only person responsible for how I spend my time. When I made the conscious decision to make myself a priority and gave myself permission to be selfish with my time, I was happier. I enjoyed the time I carved out to reflect and contemplate.

Expectations are essential to setting boundaries.

Are you setting clear expectations with yourself?
With your spouse or significant other?
Work? Children? Friends? Volunteer organizations? Family members?
Do your expectations ever change?

I found my personal expectations changed significantly when I went from being an employee to owning my own business. At the very time I was investing heavily in growing my business, I found I didn't have the luxury of investing in other relationships, including the relationship with myself. One of the first things I relied on was setting boundaries to ensure I was managing the limited time available to me. This wasn't easy to do. I'll admit I still struggle with this aspect. I continue to reflect on my needs and make a concerted effort to communicate what I am capable of accomplishing, both personally and professionally. Soon others understood and respected my expectations and boundaries.

What do music and television have to do with creating space to hear important messages? You likely have similar interests that eat up your time. Maybe it isn't music or television, but rather magazines, happy hour, or bingo at the fire hall. I encourage you to spend a few minutes answering the following questions:

How do you focus on yourself?

Where do you find the most meaningful ways to create space to reflect and listen?

One of the most effective ways I found to get to know my authentic self is to spend dedicated time reflecting each and every day. It was incredibly important for me throughout my journey to create these quiet moments when I could turn off the world and listen. What was good about today? What could I have done better? Did I handle myself with integrity and courage today? Did I love myself today? How can I do better tomorrow? Who hurt me today? How can I protect myself better tomorrow?

I encourage you to be selfish with your time. You may enjoy meditation or your version of meditation may be taking a nap. Challenge yourself to find fifteen minutes each day to spend in quiet contemplation. Who among us can't spare fifteen minutes on ourselves? If you aren't willing to invest in yourself you can't expect anyone else to be willing to do so.

In order to truly reinvent yourself you need to get to know yourself. This means deliberately spending quiet time with your innermost thoughts. It won't be easy. You may feel selfish and that is okay. Allow yourself to uncover the layers you've assumed over the past several years. Part of the joy of reinventing yourself is the discovery of the real you. Get comfortable hearing your innermost thoughts. Give them the power and freedom they deserve.

Women are taught from a very early age to embrace everyone and get along. We are rewarded for having the most friends and being popular. We are discouraged from being exclusionary. We are supposed to be nice, sweet and kind to everyone. Unfortunately this sets women up for failure. If we let everyone in, we will have neither the time nor the desire to nurture ourselves.

I learned some of the most fulfilled women I know set boundaries, most often out of necessity and in reaction to limits on their schedule. Again, I wish I learned this sooner in my life. When you set appropriate boundaries with people, you empower yourself to be successful. I caution you to embrace boundary-setting sooner rather than later. Without appropriate boundaries, your journey to redesign your life will be significantly delayed and potentially unsuccessful.

Now you have the time to hear the important messages in your life. How do you determine what qualifies as important? Potential worries are: What if nothing comes from my meditation? Is it possible my journey of redefinition is already a bust? Be patient. Give yourself time. It took me three years to hear the message to start my own business. Things happen in their own time. You cannot control the timing of your journey. You can do your best to drive change in your life, however life's messages are organic and come to you in their own time.

I found I kept hearing the same message over and over. First it was a faint thought. *Wow, she runs her own business. I wonder if I could ever do that. No, not something I'm capable of doing.* **A year later I'd run into another person who would tell me I should start my own business. I'd dream about owning my own company. What would I do? What would I call my company? How would I grow my business?** *I'm not good at business development so I could never own my own business.* **Two months later I'd meet another woman entrepreneur and she would encourage me to consider starting my own business.**

65

This was life's way of nudging me. But since I was not open to hearing the messages, life got more aggressive and hit me over the head. Then I understood it was an important message and ready or not here it was! Previously I was not open to hearing the messages. It wasn't until I finally put all the messages together and was open to listening to life that I truly found the ideal position. And all those doubts faded away.

What if you don't like the messages being heard? Do you have to listen to them? Of course not. You are in the driver's seat. You control your destiny. Continue to create space to hear life's messages. I found when I would journal I got significantly more out of my sessions. I would write down ideas, thoughts, and images. Then I was able to reflect on the specific themes or concepts presented over and over again. How do you channel your creativity? Consider what mediums work best for you. Try several and see which works.

In order to let go of the status quo you need to invest in yourself. There is no better investment than you. It may seem selfish at first. You may not get the support you deserve. Persevere. Schedule time every day to reflect and simply disengage. Eventually you will get comfortable with the quiet. Then you will hear the messages. And then you can continue your journey. Why not give yourself time to reflect and discover the message life is offering you? I promise you won't be disappointed!

CREATING SPACE

We've got so much competing for our attention that it's easy to put ourselves last. Schedule quiet time, whether this means actual meditation or an activity that is meditative for you, like walking alone, hiking, running, yoga or stretching, following a labyrinth, baking, or doing crafts or creative activities.

Sometimes when we are in the shower or washing dishes, we get our greatest insights and ideas. Our minds are shut off and relaxed so our "greater mind," our intuition and ideas can get through. These allow you to make the big, joyful leaps in your life. Invest time in activities that you enjoy, even if it means sitting in a lawn chair on a summer's day with a cool drink. It's possible that this could be the most important part of your day and most likely what you'll remember about today a month from now.

Creating space is vitally important. Once you schedule activities, hold to your boundaries. These are actual scheduled boundaries. Make sure everyone knows that your quiet time or your leisure activities are to be respected. Ask yourself how much energy you have to give to your family or your business if you are irritated, depleted, angry or upset? Any task or encounter you approach from a happy, calm and centered state will always go better.

Keep these suggestions in mind:

- Slow down and pay attention. Are you rushing? Don't let your life become a blur. Continually call yourself back to the present. You may want to wear a bracelet or some amulet that reminds you of being in the moment.

- Acknowledge your feelings. Don't push them away even if they are uncomfortable. This is important information because feelings can tell us "yes" or "no."

- Decide how you want to nurture yourself, and create space in your life for you. Make it pleasurable.

- Schedule your self-nurturing activities and honor that time as you would a business appointment or your child's doctor's appointment.

- When you schedule for the year, put in your vacations first. When you schedule for the month, schedule out your quiet time, your inspiration time, your idea time.

- Trust your instincts.

Ask Yourself:

- What was good about today?

- What could I have done better?

- What are my personal values?

- What made me happy today?

- How did I stretch out of my comfort zone today?

- What one thing will I do differently tomorrow?

- What messages am I hearing from the external environment (from things like overhearing conversations, music, etc.) and what are they telling me?

CHAPTER 4:
FAILURE IS NOT AN OPTION

This chapter is about answering the question, "What would you do if you knew you could not fail?" and then doing it. As you let go of your status quo, you want to have the utmost confidence that not only is your success inevitable and failure not an option, but you cannot fail. Failing would mean not honoring your need to let go of the status quo. It would mean remaining where you are because you do not believe in your ability to succeed. We know you can succeed and are confident your success is imminent. Failure really isn't an option because when you let go of what's not working in your life and step into where you are meant to be, your success is inevitable. Are you ready to let yourself achieve success?

—Julie & Andria

71

Julie's Story

BABY BUMPS IN THE ROAD

Twenty years from now you will be more disappointed by the things that you didn't do than by the ones you did do so throw off the bowlines. Sail from the safe harbor. Catch the trade winds in your sails. Explore. Dream. Discover. —Mark Twain

High achiever, driven, motivated, goal-oriented. These were the labels I heard growing up. My family valued a strong work ethic, achievement and a stellar personal reputation. My father served America as a career naval officer. My mother not only worked as a full-time civil servant, but while I was in high school but she also was an English-as-a-second-language instructor while we lived in Japan. Self-reliance and independence were developed early in my family. I am fortunate to benefit from these values and can appreciate the significant role they played in shaping my authentic self.

Remember the dream job I got and lost? At the exact moment I learned I was officially unemployed, I began to hear the doubting internal monologue. _"You weren't good enough for that position. You thought you could handle it and clearly you couldn't. You're not smart enough for that position and they figured it out before you even started the job."_ Instead of giving in to the messages as I usually did, I quickly stopped the monologue. Obviously the employment decision was outside of my control. I would never understand what factors led the company to eliminate my position. In that very moment I realized I could only control how I would react to the situation. I was not going to let the negative dialogue define me. I wasn't even going to allow those negative thoughts to occur.

This was life's way of hitting me over the head with a message I wasn't listening to along my journey. I was faced with an opportunity to tap in to my inner entrepreneur and, despite my initial fear, I embraced the chance and dove into the deep end of the pool.

In that very moment of defeat, my company, Human Capital Strategic Consulting (HCSC), was born. All the same questions I had when Andria and I met earlier were still present, however they didn't seem quite as daunting. When faced with a blank sheet of paper, the option of starting a business didn't terrify me so much. Failure wasn't an option. I would create success!

I drew upon my work ethic, positive reputation and professional network to start a business from the ground up. I wasn't going to pay attention to the statistics—10 percent unemployment, 33 percent of new businesses fail within the first two years, and only 44 percent make it four years. These were meaningless to me.

What did I have to lose? The only thing I couldn't live with was not trying. I wouldn't give up without a fight. Failure to me was not living up to my fullest potential. If I failed trying, at least I tried. Would I regret doing this or would I regret NOT doing this more? Not creating Human Capital Strategic Consulting would be one of my biggest regrets. If I didn't get clients and wasn't able to build the business, I knew I could try again to find a full-time job. Yes, it would be difficult but certainly not impossible.

I wanted to build a business that provided meaningful value to my clients along with personalized service. Knowing at least an aspect of what I wanted to do differently from the status quo was critical to my definition of success. When I solicited Andria's advice regarding the possibility of starting my own business, I couldn't articulate how I was going to let go of the status quo from a work perspective. It took the events of the fall of 2010 to crystallize my goals.

I had faith in the bigger plan for me. I'd built a positive reputation, had a strong professional network, and obtained my master's degree in human resources as well as my professional certification. On paper I had the qualifications of an external human resources consultant. The only ingredient missing was having the belief in myself to serve in the consultant capacity.

When I considered opening my own business previously, it wasn't lack of self-confidence that stopped me. But on December 2nd, 2010 when the rug was pulled out from my corporate HR career, it became the lighthouse guiding me through the storm. I knew I was capable and would not let the opportunity pass me by without at least giving it my all. Going back to work for someone else was simply not something I wanted to pursue. I knew the two people I could rely on were Greg and myself. He had the confidence in me and with his support I was able to commit to my new path.

The ability to identify what was motivating me and the knowledge that my authentic self was assisting me helped me to make the decision to let go of the professional status quo and start Human Capital Strategic Consulting. There was also nothing like a mortgage payment to motivate me! I set milestones for success along the path.

At first it was simply to articulate my value proposition. Then I was able to attend a few networking events and practice business development. Again I found myself leveraging my networks and was met with endless support. People were able to give me the reassurance I needed to continue on the path to entrepreneurship. As winter wore on, despite the cold weather, I found warmth in the local business community.

Three months into my new business venture I had three clients. I was attending networking events and reconnecting with people I'd not seen in years. This was certainly the path I was supposed to be on and I simply needed a push in the right direction. The success I felt in the first six months of HCSC was like nothing I'd ever imagined. This was the "something more" I'd been seeking. I'd arrived at my professional Shangri-La and it was so much better than I could have ever imagined, even if I found it by accident.

As I would experience over and over again, the lessons I learned on my journey were demonstrated in both the professional and personal aspects of my life. Failure wasn't simply a lesson applied to my career, I also had to learn it in another very personal way.

After Greg and I decided to start a family in the spring of 2009, I naively assumed it would be easy. Unfortunately that wasn't the case. Before I knew it a full year passed without any success.

I was getting older and each month that passed was a stark reminder of the decreasing odds we would get pregnant. Initially, like many couples in our situation, Greg and I were comfortable letting nature run its course. We relished our vacations and free time knowing they would come to an end in the near future. However, as the months went on without conceiving a baby, I found myself becoming increasingly more emotional. This was one of the first times in my life I couldn't work harder to fix the problem. It was out of my control and I hated that feeling.

It was difficult for me to fake enthusiasm when a friend would tell me she was pregnant. Eventually I began to decline baby shower invitations because it was too painful to see other women experience something I so desperately wanted. While I was genuinely happy for them, selfishly I struggled, wondering what was wrong with me that we couldn't have a baby. Deep down I knew we'd be parents eventually, but the process of discovering *how* was excruciating.

After a year without success, Greg and I decided we needed some additional data to fully understand why we weren't able to conceive. It wasn't easy to make the decision to undergo fertility testing, however we needed to gather the facts. I found a few women who underwent it and peppered them with questions. At each point along the way, Greg demonstrated what a fantastic partner I had on this journey. We decided to eat the elephant one bite at a time. I honestly couldn't have made it through the testing and diagnosis process without Greg. Life was teaching me another valuable lesson in showing me what a true partner I had in him.

Fortunately, there was nothing found in the testing that medically prevented us from being able to get pregnant. So back to the drawing board we went. Why weren't we having any success? Was it my age? Stress from work? Timing? For one of the first times in our lives, Greg and I had no control over something that was so important to us.

Our answer was to decompress for two weeks in Hawaii. There is nothing like a beautiful island vacation to set things straight. And boy did they! After we returned from the vacation were elated to learn we were pregnant! Success after such a long time trying felt really good. We simply chalked it up to stress and began to enjoy the idea of being parents. How exciting to know we would welcome our first child into the world in April of 2011. We began planning, as only two type A personalities can, all the details of this exciting chapter of our lives.

Since we started down the path of partnering with a fertility specialist, we thought it best to confirm things with him. As luck would have it, my sister, Kristi, and her toddler, Jack, were in town for a few days in late August of 2010. I went through a battery of diagnostic testing to calibrate the pregnancy. One morning I visited the doctor to get a routine blood draw and confirm that my levels were rising as expected. We had no reason to believe anything but the best news would result from this standard blood test.

We were enjoying the sunny afternoon at a park when my cell phone rang. I recognized the number as the doctor's office and was prepared to hear the reassuring voice of the nurse communicating numbers (which I didn't fully understand), but I was surprised to hear the doctor was on the phone. That should have been my first clue.

As he began to speak it became clear to me this wasn't a typical follow-up call. He began by saying my numbers were down dramatically from the previous test which had only been a few days prior. Everything went quiet around me. He continued to say this was likely an indication I would miscarry. Then everything went black. He said 30 percent of women miscarry before having their first child. Finally he recommended I come back in for another test in two days. Then he offered his condolences and the call was over.

Just like that, at a beautiful park with laughing kids surrounding me, I found out I was not going to be a mom. The little life inside me was simply not to be. As I dissolved into tears, Kristi, as she had done my entire life, picked up the pieces. Jack, a sensitive soul himself, came over to see what was wrong with Auntie Julie. "Why are you crying, Auntie? Did you fall down and hurt yourself?" Such innocence and compassion only caused me to cry harder. Kristi explained to Jack I wasn't feeling well and as quickly as possible she guided both of us back to the car.

Without missing a beat, Kristi got behind the wheel of my car and drove us home. Before I could even realize what was happening, Kristi had me upstairs in bed and she was making dinner. By the grace of

God I received this devastating news when she was in town. Kristi and I live across the country from one another and don't have the luxury of being together more than a few times a year. Now she was able to physically care for me in the darkest hours of my life. She allowed me to process the news, talk when I needed to talk, cry when I needed to cry, and eventually, day by day, understand that life does go on and it will get better.

She gave me permission to feel the authentic emotions of losing a child and gave me the will to continue down the path to parenthood when I didn't think I could go on. She nurtured and cared for me as she had done my entire life.

In a matter of one week we went from planning for our first child to mourning the loss. Without the support of Greg and Kristi, I would not have survived. Jack served as the sweet soul he was by drawing me pictures and distracting me from the reality of the news. He gave me strength to continue. I wouldn't give up the dream of parenthood. We simply had to get through these dark days to enjoy the sunshine.

I cannot emphasize enough how isolated and alone I felt. At this point in my life I didn't have any friends who discussed infertility. Nobody I knew ever talked about miscarrying. I found myself, a natural extrovert, reluctant to socialize. The idea of spending time with other people talking about sports, current events or politics seemed trivial. Plus, I would break down at the sight of a baby. To say I was an emotional wreck is an understatement.

Initially I couldn't share the news of our miscarriage with anyone because I had to give myself time to process the sadness. Yes, I was grateful I wasn't farther along in my pregnancy. Yes, I knew it was a good sign that at least we knew we could get pregnant. Still, nothing seemed to dull the ache in my heart for the loss of the child we would never know. I know there is always going to be a place in my heart for the sweet baby who left us far too early. The Aries child I carried for far too short a period of time is the angel who brought me through the darkness. The silver lining was how much Greg and I grew together as we braved this journey as a couple.

Every time I recall losing our first child I am transported back to that exact moment and I feel the emotions just as intensely, regardless of how much time has passed. I vividly remember wanting concrete answers. *How can this be happening to me? What did I do to cause this to happen? Maybe this is God's way of punishing me for not wanting kids for so many years. Perhaps I don't deserve to be a parent.* The self-doubt and blame seemed endless. Unfortunately I realized there were some questions that would remain unanswered indefinitely. I will never understand why we lost our first child. I simply had to accept that this was part of my journey.

Further isolating was our inability to share our infertility story. Within a three-day timeframe we found out we were pregnant and then we also learned the baby wasn't viable. I was suffocating with the knowledge I would soon miscarry the sweet baby we yearned to have. Greg and I were forced to deal with the devastating news of an impending miscarriage. As with this whole journey, I learned more about biology than I honestly ever cared to know. Medical science was able to alert us to the pregnancy very early on, which was good. However it also was able to notify us the fetus wasn't viable as the associated hormone levels were falling instead of rising. Therefore, my body would spontaneously miscarry the baby.

Now came waiting for the other shoe to drop. I knew my body would begin to reject the baby; I simply didn't know when it would occur. Knowing I was walking around with a baby who wouldn't live long was torture. Each day I waited in agony to see the visual reminder of my inability to successfully carry a baby to term. Ten days after the happiest day of our lives, learning we were pregnant, our sweet baby died. Despite my best efforts to live a healthy life, I was left with the reminder of my inability to become a mother. My heart ached for the loss of the child I would never know. Was it a boy or girl? Would he or she look like Greg or me? Blue eyes or green? Alas, this sweet soul wasn't destined to join us and the loss was like nothing I'd ever felt before or since.

As with many women who suffer a miscarriage, I found the news too painful to share so I was primarily alone. I felt extremely responsible for not being able to properly nurture the life entrusted to me. Of course I understand now that miscarriages happen and there isn't always a reason identified. I gave myself permission to process this in whatever way worked best for me. I was selfish with this news. Sharing this extremely devastating news with even my closest friends was far too painful. Now, with the passing of time and healing, when I hear stories of other women losing a pregnancy, I find it cathartic. There is something about learning someone else's story that unites women who have lost a child.

It is a sad comfort when you learn you are not alone on your journey. I only wish I had the strength to be more candid during my own grieving process. I think I would have benefited from counseling rather than handling it independently. One of the reasons I wrote this book is to serve as a resource for other women who may be experiencing loss and infertility. Please know you aren't alone.

I didn't let the miscarriage or loss of my ideal job define me. Yes, they were devastating experiences. I honestly didn't know how I would survive. I can say for certain I'm stronger than I ever knew I could be and I have deeper faith each and every day.

HCSC was created because I was willing to listen to my inner voice and took a chance. And I didn't let the miscarriage derail my dreams of becoming a mother. Your reasons for letting go of the status quo are unique to you. Give yourself permission to be different from the crowd. Truly embracing letting go of the status quo starts with embracing your authentic self. Knowing who you are at the core of your soul is instrumental on this journey of self-reinvention. The status quo of my career path was changed for me without my permission but I eventually learned, along my journey, that this was the way I needed it to unfold. Losing a child only strengthened my desire to be a parent. It was a valuable lesson and one I honor daily.

Andria's Story

LIVING WITH CONFIDENCE

My parents placed a strong emphasis on education. My dad continually stressed the importance of good grades, getting into a good college and earning an advanced degree. Because I loved school and loved learning, this was an easy formula for me. And because I internalized most of what my parents said, I knew without a doubt that because I got good grades in high school and completed both a bachelor's and master's degree, I would be successful no matter what. This held true for me throughout my college years and beyond. I never doubted my ability to achieve anything—as long as I focused my time and attention on it, I knew I could do it.

After getting my master's degree, I had no doubt I'd be able to land a good job. And when it was time to move beyond my first job in human resources, I was confident I'd successfully compete for and obtain a position in a large corporation. All of this came to pass. I internalized so much of what I heard as a child that this is exactly what I focused on and exactly what I obtained.

When I decided I wanted to play by different rules and start my own business, I no longer had a recipe for success. I actually had the opposite. I didn't know what it took to start and run a successful business. I heard so many messages about how hard it was to be a business owner, how long it took to create a successful business and that the recession did not bode well for start-ups. I was told about the number of new businesses that fail and how risky it was to do what I was doing. I had many fearful moments and moments of doubt. *Am I doing the right thing? What if this is a mistake? What if I'm better off staying where I am, in my corporate job?*

82

When I got past the fear and doubt, which were based on what other people were saying, I reached my own inner truth which told me that yes, I was doing the right thing and the only mistake would be staying where I was out of fear. Although it might take a while to get things up and running, I knew I would be a success no matter what because I had my lifelong internal belief on my side—that belief that I could be successful at whatever I focused my time and energy on. However, even with my confidence boosted, the fear crept back in: *But what if I fail?* The answer to that was simple: failure was not an option. Furthermore, failure would actually be better than the status quo. Sounds contradictory doesn't it?

At that point in my life, I knew that staying at my corporate job and remaining in the status quo was not possible. So starting my own business with the possibility of failing actually felt like a better option than remaining where I was. The possibility of failure was an easier pill to swallow than remaining stuck where I was. Yet at the same time I knew failure would not be an option for me because even if I failed at some aspect of starting my own business, I believed it would lead me to succeed in another area. Internally I knew that success would come to me because I felt it in my bones; I would achieve my goals no matter how many roadblocks, mistakes or failures I experienced along the way. This belief in myself prevailed over all the naysayers and even my own doubting self-talk. I could not deny my internal, engrained belief in my own ability to succeed.

Where does self-belief come from? For me, I know it started with listening to my dad tell me that as long as I followed the prescribed recipe for success, I could not fail. Internalizing that, I continued to experience proof of it throughout my life. I analyzed it enough to know that although I was doing what I was told I should do to be successful (going to school to get my degrees, working hard in my jobs to continue to grow my career), I was also incredibly focused on my fruitful results. I realized that it was my own commitment and focus that attributed to my accomplishments more than the fact that I was playing by a prescribed set of rules. Knowing that and seeing the proof of it continued to fuel my belief in myself. My achievements really weren't about the prescribed set of rules, they were about my own belief that I would succeed.

I have always been a very strong-willed person. Some of it comes from sheer stubbornness and some of it comes from a strong desire to prove things to myself. I don't take commitments lightly nor do I say things I don't mean. When I commit to doing or achieving something, it is as good as done. Whether it is a commitment to myself or to someone else, it carries the same weight. That is why it took me so long to leave my marriage and that is why when I said, aloud, that I didn't want to live in that type of marriage for the rest of my life, I knew what it meant. It meant I was making a commitment to *me* and would not let myself down.

When I left my marriage, I wasn't as sure that I'd be successful in another relationship. I had proof of success in my professional life, yet not as much in my personal life. I now had two failed marriages—not a great track record. I had no idea what having a successful relationship looked like or meant. My belief in my ability to be in a thriving relationship wasn't substantial. I had to instill that belief in other ways. The only way I could convince myself and feel strongly that I could and would be successful in my personal life after my second marriage ended was to redefine how to thrive outside of being married.

If it meant I was single for the rest of my life, I'd make that a success, and if it meant I was involved in another relationship, I'd make that a success. My definition of success in these situations was mine to create. And that was the beauty of it: I got to define what it meant for me to be a success. I set high expectations for myself but at the end of the day, the only person I was (and am) answering to was *me*.

84

After my very short first marriage failed, I had a soundtrack playing in my head that I was not a good wife. And I believed it. I knew I was career-focused and heard endless stories from others about how you cannot have both a successful career and a successful marriage or family life. I didn't believe I knew how to be a good wife. I questioned and doubted myself throughout my second marriage. I also found myself occasionally wondering how long the marriage would actually last. If that isn't a recipe for failure I'm not sure what is! In retrospect, I see that I never truly believed I could be successful in that marriage. I didn't expect to be and my lack of belief and expectation greatly influenced the result.

One of my favorite sayings is "What would you attempt to do if you knew you could not fail?" Living life based on that question opens possibilities; in fact, it creates infinite possibilities. Yes, I was afraid to get involved in another relationship after my marriage ended because I was afraid it would fail. I knew I liked being in relationships and, despite two failed marriages, fully believed in the institution of marriage (with the right person!).

After a rocky first year in my relationship with Matt, I began to think about that quote. *If I knew I could not fail, would I jump into this relationship with Matt with my whole heart?* Of course I would! If I knew I wouldn't fail, I wouldn't be afraid of what would happen if it didn't work out. This was a huge realization for me. I had to let go of my fear of failing so that I could actually succeed in this area of my life. In this context, the definition of success meant allowing myself to open my heart up 100 percent while letting go of my fear of failing.

Letting go of the fear of failure enabled me to re-create my belief that I could be successful in a relationship. The impact of my two failed marriages and the fear of being divorced again was like carrying an elephant on my back. It weighed me down and dragged down our

85

relationship. I had to let this go before I could truly believe in my ability to succeed as a partner to Matt. I had to redefine what that meant and internalize the new belief that although there may be bumps along the way, I would succeed and "we" would succeed. Without this self-belief, I don't know if our relationship would have survived beyond year one.

Self-belief is an essential aspect of reinventing yourself and letting go of the status quo. It will determine your actions and your results. If you do not believe in yourself and are approaching some aspect of your life with the attitude that you'll never succeed, how motivated will you be to take action? Not very. If you are certain of your success and are approaching an aspect of your life knowing you will not fail, chances are you will be much more inspired to do whatever is necessary to be successful.

Knowing I would do whatever it took to ensure my success as a business owner and in my personal life helped build my self-confidence. Think about it: If you hear someone say, "I'll do whatever it takes to make this work," you will likely think, "She is pretty determined to make it happen!" Even saying those words gives an internal confidence boost.

During the process of letting go of your status quo, you may be re-creating your life to be something different than what others may expect. This is where self-belief is critical. You must be confident in your ability to stand firm in your desire, not only to create a newly defined lifestyle for yourself (as defined by you and only you), but also to have enough confidence in what you are doing that you can ignore what everyone else thinks and says.

Years ago I clipped this quote by Michael Ignatieff from a magazine and it's hanging on a bulletin board in my office today:

One of the greatest feelings in life is the conviction that you have lived the life you wanted to live—with the rough and the smooth, the good and the bad—but yours, shaped by your own choices and not someone else's.

That essentially defines how I approached re-creating my life after I got divorced, when I left my corporate job, and as I continue to grow in life today. I am committed to living the life I want and accepting all the good and bad that comes along with my choices because they are *my* choices. I make them in my own best interest, not based on what I assume others think I should be doing.

Some people (perhaps some of you reading this) may think this sounds selfish. It may be, but one of the things I realized through my continuous evolution is that making choices that go against my own best interest or making decisions that don't resonate with me ends up negatively impacting those around me as well. It is only when I make the choices that are best for me that I'm able to give freely to others and be the best person I am. This ultimately is good for everyone.

I didn't always know this and I certainly didn't always practice this. Like many women, I was raised to put my own interests last, to make sure that everyone else around me was okay before checking to see if I was okay. But the airlines have it right when they say, "Put your own oxygen mask on before assisting others." After all, how can you help someone else if you have no air to breathe yourself? It makes the same amount of sense in your own life. How can you be anything to anyone else if you don't have enough of your own energy?

I remember when I decided to leave my marriage and then my job. Despite how scared I was, it felt like a huge exhale. Relief! Before I made those decisions, I felt like I was holding my breath and not letting enough air flow through. I didn't realize it at the time but I was cutting myself off from the possibilities of becoming what I was truly meant to be. Perhaps in society's eyes and in the eyes of those from whom I was seeking approval staying married and in the high-paying secure job was the right thing to do.

But what it meant for me was restriction. What good can I be to anyone else if I am living a restricted existence? By finally deciding to act in my own best interest, the air started to flow again and that enabled me to grow and blossom, projecting a much better version of *me* to everyone around me.

I believe that in life we get what we give. I had nothing to give of myself when I was living a life that was out of alignment with what I truly wanted. Was I concerned about what others would think? Of course I was! I had a constant tape playing in my head that said, "What will other people say? What will they think?" But I had to get over it. It didn't matter what choice I made then, or what I do today, I'll never be able to control what other people say and think! (If only...!) Plus I had made "What other people think about you is none of your business" my motto—and still recite it to myself regularly.

Anais Nin wrote, "We see things not as they are, we see things as we are." People see you from their perspective and their filter, which really has nothing to do with you. Is perception a reality? Yes, it is the perceiver's reality—not yours. Getting comfortable in my own skin, in knowing that I must do right by me before I can do right by anyone else, and knowing that what other people think of me, what I do, and what choices I make is really none of my business have allowed me to put myself first, regardless of what society says. Reminding myself of all of these things helped foster the self-belief required for me to continue on my journey.

As I mentioned earlier, when I started my own business, there were many naysayers. I was breaking the rules of the game, giving up my great corporate job, going against the grain and making a decision to create a professional life defined and designed by me. Scary? Absolutely. Exhilarating? You bet! Easy to succumb to what others think and say? Always. But I didn't. I listened to *me*.

This doesn't mean you should or must isolate yourself from others' opinions. It just means you should trust your own more than anyone else's. You should be strong enough to be true to your convictions and go after what it is you want, as defined by *you*. It's about believing in yourself enough to ignore what anyone else says and thinks. Whether other people believe in you or not does not matter. Whether *you* believe in you makes all the difference in the world.

This was one of the most critical factors in my ability to live my life, designed by me. If I did not believe I could do it, I know I would not have done it. I would have backed out and retreated into the safety net of what I knew worked, what others said worked, and what was acceptable. Not that anything I did was unacceptable, but walking away from a high-paying, high-level job at a company where I was on the fast track looked pretty stupid to any average outsider. And leaving marriage number two was probably more unacceptable to me than to anyone else. It took me much longer to gain confidence about succeeding in another relationship than it did to feel confident about starting my own business.

Building up my self-confidence was key to my success in another relationship. It all starts with self-belief. Your certainty about how successfully you can redesign your own life determines the outcome.

How can you develop this self-belief? Look back on your own life and where you have been the most successful. Think about what contributed most to your achievements and do what you can to re-create that type of momentum in your life today. What processes did you follow? How confident were you in your ability to succeed? Were thoughts of failure even present? Oftentimes we realize that times when we were most successful included the belief and expectation that we would *not* fail.

FAILURE IS NOT AN OPTION

What do you believe about yourself and your ability to be successful?

If you lack self-belief, then it's important to generate it so you can move forward and create the life you are meant to have. Generating self-belief may seem like a large task, but we have all been successful with this at various times in our lives. Reach back to those times and remember what it felt like. Tap in to those feelings and attributes. Re-create them as much as you can until they become a part of what you are doing today. Use affirmations and start speaking as if you are that person you are trying to create.

A belief is just a thought you keep thinking, so what are the thoughts you've been thinking that have created your beliefs about yourself? Are they even your thoughts or are they things that were said to you by someone at a vulnerable or impressionable time in your life?

Don't look at your past; you don't live there anymore. Look ahead and know, without a doubt, that you can and will create exactly what you desire. Another way to say this is: "Don't look back, you aren't going that way. Instead, turn towards where you want to head and focus your attention and energy on that." Believe in yourself and your inevitable success. We promise you will end up pleasantly surprised at what you can do with that self-belief fueling you.

As Henry Ford once said, "Whether you believe you can or you can't, you are right."

Journal:

- Take an introspective look at what you believe about yourself and your ability to be successful.

- Where did these beliefs come from? Are they serving you? If not, what new beliefs would serve you?

- Which voices have you internalized? When you're criticizing yourself, really listen. Is it your mother's voice? Your father's?

- Recall times when you have been successful. Re-create these feelings and attributes in what you are doing today. You may even close your eyes, call up a memory and feel it before you make an important phone call.

- Remember what anyone else thinks of you is none of your business, it's theirs. What they say or think is a reflection of *them* that they're projecting on *you.*

- Make building self-confidence your #1 priority. Congratulate yourself for the smallest accomplishment, celebrate the milestones and appreciate yourself for how well you're doing and how much you've grown.

Ask Yourself:

- What experience did I learn the most from and why?(It's best not to label them "good" or "bad," but instead look at the expanded perspective you gained from them.)

- What significant obstacle have I overcome?

- What did I learn in the process of rebounding?

- How can I apply the lesson to future situations?

- What barriers exist in my life that prevent me from moving forward?

- Whose rules am I playing by? (If they are not your own, *create* new rules that work best in your life. Write down three new rules today.)

CHAPTER 5:
THE POWER OF YOUR PEOPLE

As women, many of us have the tendency to take on too much and do more than we truly can (or should). We don't readily ask for help, despite how much we may need and want it. We are conditioned to believe that asking for help is a sign of weakness. As you move along your journey to let go of the status quo, you cannot do it alone. We've tried it alone and it wasn't pretty! You can try, but you will inevitably need the support of other people. Learn from our missteps. This element is about the importance of having a strong support system in your life, not only as you are making big changes, but at all times.

It's about recognizing when you need help from others and being able to ask for it. It's about knowing who your supporters and #1 fans are and having them by your side cheering you on as you move along your journey. It's about setting boundaries with those who shouldn't have unlimited access to you. Your network of supporters is vital to your success and your well-being. Many of you probably already know this, but for those who do not, as you explore this element you will truly discover how powerful your people can be and how critical they are to smoothing the journey to let go of the status quo.

—Julie & Andria

Andria's Story

Support *tr.v.* To hold in position so as to keep from falling, sinking, or slipping. To keep from weakening or failing. Strengthen."

—thefreedictionary.com

TAKE COMFORT FROM THE TRIBE

Think about who and what you use as support in your life. Different situations typically require different support structures and systems. Letting go of the status quo can require a whole slew of support systems that range from chocolate to wine to vodka (or whatever your drink of choice may be) to fierce exercise (or fierce lounging) to the people who pull you up when it's required and also let you crumble when necessary.

Each type of support system is vital. Think of what you do or who you call when you want to celebrate something or when you've gotten the wind knocked out of you. These are your support systems. Now think of who is still standing or what has revealed itself after a life-changing event. These are your new support systems to help you usher in your new life. They might be the same as the originals or they might look totally different—it doesn't matter. What matters is that you have them.

I grew up in an Italian family. We aren't a big family but it doesn't really take many Italians to seem like a lot. I only have one sister and a handful of cousins, but put us all in a room with aunts, uncles, parents, and grandparents and there might as well be one hundred of us. We are loud, loyal, loving, passionate, and like to be in each other's business. Growing up and to this day, my sister Debra is the closest person to me. Like many siblings, we grew up loving each other one moment and arguing the next. And we still have that pattern today. She is my toughest critic and my biggest supporter. In fact, I have come to realize that all my family members are some of my biggest supporters.

Today I know that having a support system is a vital piece to succeed and survive in life. However, for a good part of my life I resisted support. I was (and in many regards, still am) fiercely independent. I have been independent to a fault and know exactly what influenced my sense of needing to be so self-sufficient.

My parents got divorced when I was thirteen years old. The impact of the divorce was a critical part of my journey. When my parents separated, my mom was devastated. Like many families back in the 1970s and 1980s, she was a stay-at-home mom and did everything to support my dad's successful career. He was climbing the corporate ladder and we, as a family, went where his career took him.

When their marriage ended, I saw my mom fall apart. She was in pieces, and understandably so, since life as she knew it and planned it was suddenly gone. As a very impressionable young teen, I remember the exact thought I had, repeatedly, as I witnessed her devastation. It was: "I will never, ever, in my life be that dependent on any one person."

What I interpreted was that my mom's dependence on my dad caused her tremendous pain and loss. I didn't understand the full ramification of why she was experiencing such loss but I swore to myself, at age thirteen, that I would never enable anyone or anything to cause me to fall apart like she did. Of course, I fell apart in my own unique ways, but I was true to that promise and never felt a sense of dependence on anyone.

That also meant I didn't ask for help and had a pretty thick wall up around me, which said to others, "I got it. I'm fine. I don't need you."

This can be and was a standoffish way to live. The few I let close to me (even those I actually married), encountered a wall around me. I let that interpretation of my mom's pain have a profound impact on the way I lived for a good part of my life. The impact was deep and it took years for me to let it go.

The older I got and the more my life evolved, the more I realized how much I actually needed others as supporters and that having a support system was a vital part of being successful. I also realized that it's impossible to have a fulfilling relationship with anyone without the give and take of supporting each other. Today, I still would describe myself as very independent, though I am much more willing to ask for and accept help when I am at a loss and need the help of others. It may take me a bit longer to actually admit it or ask for it, but the fact that I do ask and allow myself to receive has meant big growth for me.

It is true that you find out who your true supporters are during your darkest hours. With the exception of my parents and Debra, I always assumed my extended Italian family would judge me for my two divorces simply because loyalty and commitment were huge family values. That was an unfair assumption because although I am not as close with my extended family today as I was growing up, I always received a tremendous amount of unconditional support from them— regardless of the life changes that were occurring. My parents and Debra have always been my anchors. I know my family members (both immediate and extended) are some of my biggest supporters—they always have been and continue to be. Regardless of circumstances, they always had my back. I wouldn't trade the strong loyalty of our Italian family for anything.

I have never had a lot of friends. I am a big introvert, always have been. I used to be called shy but it was not shyness. I like people. I enjoy being around them and am confident and comfortable—I'm just introverted. This doesn't mean that I can't be extroverted and social. It means that I recharge my batteries and get more energy being alone or with small groups than being in crowds or in overly social situations.

When I was growing up and in school, I was careful about choosing friends. I didn't allow a lot of people into my personal space, so always only had a few very good, close friends. My closest and truest friend has always been, and still is, Smith, who was also my roommate in college. From the moment she walked up and introduced herself at our college freshman orientation (a divine day I will always remember), she has been a pillar of strength and support for me. She is as close to me as Debra and, along with my Mom, is the person I can call at 3:00 a.m. when life seems a bit scary or I have a fun, crazy story or dream to share. Yes, she is THAT person and is the type of friend everyone should be blessed to have.

Do you have a friend like that? I'm sure as you are reading this, you are thinking of the people in your life (or those things in your life) that are your support systems. I know that I wouldn't be where I am today without the strength of my supporters. I have a primary "tribe" of three and, that's what I call them: my tribe. They are (as you probably can guess) Debra, Smith, and my mom.

I've always been incredibly attached to my mom. I was the kid hanging on her leg when she'd be trying to drop me off at kindergarten, or sitting outside the bathroom door while she was in there (my poor mother…).

After butting heads throughout high school, like so many moms and daughters, my mom became my friend when I went away to college. That is an interesting dynamic, because she is always Mom first but I also feel incredibly blessed to be able to call her my friend. I know she, like Debra, would defend me to the end of time.

These are the three I go to in all good times and bad times. They surrounded me (both physically and emotionally) when I was going through my divorces and ensured that I had all the reinforcements I needed. Even when I tried to push them away, they kept showing up. They boosted my self-esteem when it was down in the subzero range, they cooked for me, cleaned for me (yes, that was mostly my mom), and they made me laugh on days when that was probably the most unlikely possibility. They also stopped sympathizing with me and gave me a swift kick in the ass when they got tired of my "woe is me" bullshit.

The most important thing I learned from my tribe during these times is that it's okay to need help, it's okay to ask for help, and it's okay to let others know you're not okay.

Who's in your tribe? These are the people who you know, beyond a shadow of a doubt, are going to answer the phone at 3:00 a.m. when it's your number that pops up on caller ID, or are going to jump in the car or on the next plane to get to you because you need them. They are also the people who will support you through whatever decisions you make, no matter how ridiculous they seem at the time. They will never say, "I told you so" (despite the fact that they probably did, more than once) and will always be your #1 fans.

You may be familiar with the saying "People come into your life for a reason, a season, or a lifetime." Obviously my tribe falls into the "lifetime" category. But they aren't my only supporters. I have some wonderful friends whom I have known for many years who definitely fall into the lifetime category yet just aren't those I reach out to immediately. They are big supporters and I cherish those relationships deeply.

I've also had some wonderful people come into my life at just the right time and stay for a brief period. This was especially true during my divorce. While I was living in New Jersey for a short seven months, I became very close with a group of people who, although they may not have realized it, played a huge role in my entire personal reinvention. Most of them were several years younger and, because they had a different perspective on life, they helped me rediscover who I was and who I wanted to be outside of my marriage. They were in my life for an important reason. I believe people like this show up at exactly the right time and for the perfect "season."

Who are your season and reason people? Just like me, I'm sure you recognize them as being as vital as your tribe or lifetime supporters. They serve a different role but they are just as important as your other supporters.

When I started my business, I discovered an entire new network of supporters: fellow entrepreneurs and business owners. After being enclosed inside the corporate world for so many years, I had no idea what I was missing—millions of other people supporting each other! Don't get me wrong, I made a few really good friends while in my corporate life and these friends fall into the lifetime category. But they were few and far between, likely because the environment was very political and competitive. When I left to start my own business, I received tremendous support from the few friends I made there but the rest of the people I spent years working with disappeared from my life. That was (and is) perfectly fine.

Starting my own business forced me to embark on this new area of networking and developing relationships with new people. I have said this repeatedly and will continue to say it: Since launching my business, I have met the most wonderful and generous people by networking in the Washington, D.C., area. The people I have met and developed relationships with have become good friends and even better business associates. Some of them are season and reason people but many more are lifetime people. Will they be the people I call at 3:00 a.m.? I think there are one or two more whom I could definitely add to my tribe but the rest are probably thankful to be excluded.

The point is, these people have supported me from the first year of my business (when I had no idea what I was doing) until today (when I still feel uncertain in many areas). They continue to connect me to others who can help me and they encourage me to continue to follow my heart and expand my reach. If you had told me five years ago that today I would have such a strong network of supporters in my life, both business and personal, I doubt I would have believed it. I just never really thought about how important it is and how much it adds to my life. When I was starting my business, I recognized that I needed help and these are the people I go to for help. Even when my independent side rears its head, I let that go and ask for the help I need. I have never been disappointed with the results.

The unique thing about using support systems effectively is knowing when you need them and when you don't, and who you need at different times. People I thought were supporters in my corporate life have disappeared and it's the few who stuck by me that I want now in my network of supporters.

When you are going through any life change and taking steps to let go of the status quo, you need the right people to encourage you, not the naysayers who cause you to question what you are doing. Sometimes you must let go of those who keep you in the status quo. It's important to keep away from people who are fearful of what you want to do or who come up with every reason why you shouldn't do it— even if they are the lifetime friends and even if they are in your tribe. It doesn't mean they disappear from your life, you just distance

yourself for a while until you are comfortable enough with your progress that their negativity does not have an impact on you.

For example, my mom is a worrier. She worries about everything. When I was giving up my cushy corporate job, I am almost sure that she thought to herself, "What on earth is she doing? She's not married and has no one to fall back on. What if it doesn't work out?" (She never said that to me so I'm making assumptions, but the conversations I had with her drew me to this conclusion.)

She constantly told me how hard it was to start a business and how LONG it took to build a base of clients. During year one of my new business, she asked me incessantly how things were going, how much work I had, and who my clients were. I don't even know if my mom fully understood what my business was all about but she wanted to know all about my workflow.

By listening to her and having these conversations, I was soaking up a lot of her anxiety and worry—not exactly beneficial in the first year of a new business! And considering our close relationship, it wasn't easy to distance myself from her. So what did I do? I limited talk about my business. I told her everything was fine and, at one point, asked her to please stop asking me about it.

I did not want or need that type of negative energy around me as I was trying to get things up and running. Instead, I surrounded myself with supporters who built me up, encouraged me, and never said a word about how long it might take to get enough paying clients to feel comfortable. My new network of fellow entrepreneurs and successful business owners lifted me up and enabled me to get where I am today. They were (and are) the exact support system I needed for my business growth.

Sustaining these important relationships may seem time consuming but it's really quite simple. I believe we all make time for the things that are important to us. I not only make time for them, I put my heart into sustaining them and supporting the people who have been kind enough to be there for me.

If you find yourself thinking, "I don't even have time to call my current friends, let alone make new ones," I'd say it's not important to you. When you find yourself ready to make a significant life change, though, you will most certainly want those supporters in your corner, so my suggestion would be to make time for them today.

One of my many lessons when I started my business is that I wished I had grown and leveraged a larger network before I started my business. It all worked out fine, but if you already have a support system in place, you'll be that much more ahead of the game. And as you decide to let go of your status quo and redesign your life, you can call into play the people who give you energy. Not only do you want to surround yourself with those who lift you up but you also want to take advantage of opportunities to add new people to your support system. You just never know who might become a new member of your tribe.

Julie's Story

GIVING AND RECEIVING SUPPORT

As we grow up, we realize it becomes less important to have more friends and more important to have real ones. —Pinterest

I'm a proud extrovert! Not sure if it is nature or nurture, but it is something I've learned to embrace. By the time I graduated from high school I had moved seven times within the U.S. and abroad. Since we moved every few years during my childhood, I was forced to make new friends often, and unfortunately wasn't able to nurture those relationships once we relocated. My friends tell me I'm an intensely loyal friend.

When I began to let go of the status quo I found myself redefining my support system. Rather than simply accepting all the people who were in my life I began to manage my support system more strategically. What I realized along my journey was how important and valuable my support system was to my ability to live an authentic life. When I surrounded myself with people who accepted me for who I was, I found I was happier and more fulfilled.

I've developed strong friendships with a variety of women who bring amazing strength to the friendships. My tribe has many diverse personalities I wouldn't trade for the world. Lashelle calls it like it is. She is going to shoot straight and tell me the truth even if I don't want to hear it. She is the woman I can ask anything and she will give me an honest answer. She loves to laugh and isn't afraid to take a risk. She encourages me to stretch my comfort zone and manages to love me even when I can't love myself. She is the person who I can call any hour of the day and know she will answer.

105

Amy H. is the cheerleader. She is eternally optimistic and only sees people's strengths. She finds any occasion to celebrate simply for the sake of it. Everyone needs an Amy H. in her tribe—someone who will plan for the fun in life. She is thoughtful, kind and nurturing beyond measure. Early on in our friendship I found her mothering me when I needed it most. She brought light to my life during the darkest days. Without her spirit my life would be far less joyful.

How do I even begin to describe Windy? She walked alongside me, and occasionally carried me, on my path to motherhood. She accepted me without hesitation when I was child-free by choice. She shared in the anticipation of my imminent motherhood when Greg and I decided to try to have a child. She dried my tears month after month when we weren't successful in conceiving. She was one of the few people I shared our miscarriage with and she mourned the loss of our baby. Windy reinvents herself with ease and grace. She is my living wife and mother role model.

Finally there is Amy P. She is my true north. Amy has endless optimism for the human race. Amy is my fashion advisor, reality show viewing partner, sports enthusiast and girl-power role model. She dedicates her life to creating opportunities for advancement for others. I am fortunate to call her my best friend.

I hope you are fortunate to have a tribe of supporters to walk side by side with you on your journey. By surrounding yourself with people who champion you, the ride is exponentially more fun!

It is equally important to nurture and develop your *professional* support system. I worked with some amazing leaders throughout my career without even recognizing the impact they had on my professional development. Andria continues to be a huge influence professionally. She started her own business in a challenging economy and worked

106

hard for her success. She taught me to rely on my strengths and showed me how to take calculated risks. We share similar personal values, which only serves to strengthen our professional focus. She is a constant sounding board when I struggle with professional decisions and isn't afraid to remind me of the ultimate goal. She believed in my entrepreneurial dream long before I did and I'm grateful she never gave up on me!

I discovered that sometimes the person you may not expect to becomes a lifeline along your journey. Stephanie was one such individual. We connected through a networking group and our professional relationship evolved into a true friendship over the years. Stephanie was on the career fast track. She advanced quickly as organizations capitalized on her intelligence and stellar work ethic. She quickly became a mentor to me.

When I called Stephanie to share my job circumstances, she not only immediately returned my call, but she continued to serve as a source of power and strength throughout my journey. She offered her professional advice, personal compassion and spiritual support. Stephanie was truly a career emergency medical technician (EMT) in my time of need. My wish for each of you who read this book is to have a Stephanie in your life to help you along your journey of reinvention. And if you do, please remember to model this behavior to someone else down the road. You may be the emotional EMT someone else needs.

I vividly recall attending a board meeting in December of 2010 just a week after I "lost" my dream job. It was an awkward situation since this organization had ties to my old job as well as the new one I almost had. How was I supposed to communicate this situation to my peers on the board? The emotions were still so raw that I found it difficult to discuss them without breaking down in tears.

As I walked into the meeting, Steve, a leadership coach, immediately greeted me with a smile and a big hug. He sat me down right next to him. He was my "wing man" at every board meeting. He offered me endless amounts of advice about how to grow my business. Without even knowing it, Steve gave me the confidence to continue my entrepreneurial journey. He offered to leverage his network to support my professional growth. More important, he gave me permission to let down my guard and be authentic in a business setting.

Steve helped me shed one status quo I had, that of being reserved in professional settings. I naïvely thought I had to act a certain way in order to be taken seriously by those more seasoned in their careers. By virtue of being vulnerable, I found the support of my peers on the board.

The best thing about Steve was the authentic way he supported me. It never felt like an imposition when I called him. He went out of his way to offer his time and expertise. I learned, and continue to learn from him every time we interact. I've also taken the opportunity to model his supportive style in situations with others. Steve knows this is a tribute to his leadership.

My tribe wasn't created overnight. It continues to evolve daily. As I was advancing in my career, my professional network continued to grow. I kept in close contact with my former supervisors when I left my first company. I continue to be surprised by the doors that open simply because I am an alumna of that organization.

As my career progressed and I became a supervisor, I took an active role in developing team members. I took great pride in helping grow and develop the next layer of leadership. There was nothing more gratifying than seeing my colleagues shine as human resources professionals. Selfishly, it was tough for me when they left the company to take on bigger positions outside the organization.

One of my greatest moments of pride as a team leader came when I had to say farewell to two of my best team members, Jackie and Caroline. I had the privilege of working with an amazing team for two years in corporate human resources. After an exhaustive search, I hired two outstanding professionals and our internal HR team was the epitome of high performance. We shared the same work ethic, values and beliefs. We operated as a seamless team toward the common goal. It was incredible watching Jackie and Caroline grasp new technical skills and develop into confident businesswomen.

Then, one beautiful spring day, they managed to teach me a valuable life lesson: Change can be good and is often unexpected. Both of my awesome team members resigned within fifteen minutes of each other. They both realized in order to take their careers to the next level they would need to leave the organization.

And so the students taught the teacher. I was devastated, but I knew they were making the right decisions for their careers. I remain close to both and take enormous pride knowing I was a small part of their professional success. That is the thing about your tribe; if you pick the right people, you want what is best for them over what is best for you.

My tribe continues to be a source of strength on my journey of reinvention. When I am faced with a decision about a client matter, I often rely on a tribe member to bounce ideas off of and I ultimately come to the right decision with their guidance. We are amazing creatures who succeed because we support one another. We gain energy, strength and confidence from our peers. What better resource for you as you reinvent yourself?

Who do you admire? What characteristics resonate with you? Who do you know who possesses these characteristics? How can you learn from them?

It was integral for me that I could be authentic and vulnerable with the group of people I relied on. I knew I couldn't weather the choppy waters of infertility and the uncertainty of starting a business without a tribe of supporters. I couldn't have survived the miscarriage without their love and support. It often isn't until you are at your lowest point that you can fully appreciate the value of a support system.

Your tribe is unique to you just as mine is an evolving reflection of me. I encourage you to strongly consider who *shouldn't* be included. Why am I now being exclusionary? Shouldn't everyone be allowed in? As I let go of the status quo, it became apparent to me, rather quickly, that not everyone has the same goals. Not everyone can provide the level of support you need at a given point in time. Make an active decision about whom you allow into your tribe. I've found some people played a huge role in my tribe for many years, however as we each evolved we simply didn't connect anymore.

The journey of reinvention isn't for everyone. Not everyone strives to grow, change and develop. That is okay! Give yourself permission to let some relationships go. I was slow to learn this lesson and found myself resisting the messages I was meant to receive. *Did I do something wrong? Did I offend them? Why aren't we talking as candidly as we once did? What did I do to cause the relationship to change?* Instead of simply accepting the person's actions at face value, I took it upon myself to continue to invest in the relationship. STOP! If the relationship is supposed to exist it should be a mutual partnership. Not all the time, not fifty/fifty, but both parties should invest energy in nurturing the relationship.

Ask yourself, *Does this person add to my life? Do I walk away from our interactions feeling positive? Am I comfortable being my authentic self when I interact with this person?* Your tribe should be comprised of people who inspire you, believe in you and share common values, beliefs and goals. These are the people who build your self-confidence and self-worth.

Don't forget your tribe is a living being and it requires daily nurturing. The currency of your tribe is time and emotion. It isn't easy to see the immediate payoff from an investment in your support system. In order to develop deep, meaningful relationships you must be willing to give of yourself without expecting anything in return. This isn't easy but is well worth your investment.

Every person deserves a support system to rely on throughout their life, in good times and bad. The important thing to remember is that you are in control of whom you let have VIP access to you. Be selective! You are worth it!

THE POWER OF YOUR PEOPLE

If you are a maverick or an entrepreneur and challenger of the status quo, you are probably independent, but it's hard to create a business without other people—people to employ, clients/customers, and peers to reach out to for referrals, professional advice and support. And it's hard to re-create your life without other people—people to lift you up, be in your corner and lend a hand.

There is a distinction between receiving and becoming dependent. Where is that line for you?

You must become comfortable with receiving. When you receive, receive fully. You do not always have to reciprocate or feel you "owe" someone something in kind right away. Your energy exchange could be helping someone else in some way, not the person who helped you. That's the way the Universe works.

If you resist receiving, start saying yes to the little things. If you can't receive something small graciously, how can you receive the larger things such as bigger paydays? Receiving isn't a sign of weakness; it's a sign of openness and faith in yourself. Giving and receiving are a circle—one must have both to feel complete.

- Recognize that you will need people to help you at various times in your life.

- It's okay and even advisable to ask for help when you need it.

- Allow others to help you.

- Allow yourself to be vulnerable and honest. This is part of being real and authentic.

- Do what you can to sustain your cherished relationships today.

- Look for and take opportunities to develop new relationships through networking and social events.

- Know your support system will always be there for you, whether for that reason, that season, or your lifetime.

Ask Yourself:

- Who are your "tier one" tribe members?

- Who are your mentors?

- Who are your protégés?

- Who would count you as their tribe member?

- Is there anyone, a naysayer perhaps, whom you should consider removing from your tribe or support system?

- Make a list of your trusted circle and do something to show your gratitude, even if it's just a phone call to say thank you.

114

CHAPTER 6:
YOU GET WHAT YOU EXPECT
WHETHER YOU WANT IT OR NOT

This chapter is about the power of your beliefs and expectations and how they shape your journey and your destination. If you think back through your life, you will see evidence of this. Positive expectations tend to yield positive results, whereas negative expectations yield negative ones. As you move along your journey of letting go of your status quo, having positive beliefs and expectations is essential. It might seem difficult, but as you will see from the stories that follow, making a choice to be positive, have faith and expect only the best can and will have direct impact on your journey. Without fail, you will get what you expect, whether you want it or not. So why not expect the best?

—Julie & Andria

Andria's Story

When you change the way you look at things, the things you look at change.

—*Wayne Dyer*

EXPECTING THE BEST

It was my freshman year in high school, and I was sitting in the gymnasium with the rest of the students. There was some sort of pep rally occurring and a woman (I wish I could remember her name) was there to talk to the student body about the power of positive thinking. She told us that every day we can choose to be positive and happy or we can choose something else. Either way, she said, our thoughts and our attitudes will attract similar things into our lives. It made complete sense to me at the time, although I don't believe I truly embraced it beyond that day. That is my first memory about the power of positive thinking.

I was raised Catholic and would hear similar things from my mom and my grandparents, but said in a very Catholic way, such as: "Think positive things and God will walk by and say 'Amen.'" Sort of the same idea . . . right?

In those days, there wasn't a lot of positive energy in my house. While my parents were still married, I remember my dad working very hard, and being under a lot of stress because of his increasing job responsibilities with each move and each promotion. My mom, Debra and I were easily impacted by his intense moods and mostly just reacted to how he was doing. Maybe that's why, even though the message I heard from the motivational speaker in my high school gym struck me, I didn't think about it much beyond that day.

116

After my parents divorced, there was a less intense energy in our home. And I was more interested in spending time with my friends than being at home. However, my overall perspective at that time was that people's moods and frame of mind were mostly reactions to what was going on externally as opposed to being something they chose independently when they woke up in the morning.

I repeatedly met people throughout my life who seemed inherently positive; they were upbeat and their lives seemed to mirror back to them their sunny expectations and energy. But I never slowed down enough to question it beyond thinking to myself, *Why are they so upbeat all the time?*

It wasn't until I was in my thirties and broke my ankle that this idea of positive thinking reemerged as a dominant part of my life. When I was laid up, Smith suggested I read the book *Excuse Me, Your Life is Waiting* by Lynn Grabhorn. The information in the book felt like something I inherently knew—our powerful thoughts play a huge role in creating our reality—and was just being reminded of.

When I began to rediscover who I was outside of my marriage, that was the true beginning of not only living my life from this perspective of "our mindset and beliefs create our life experiences," but also adopting it as my belief system. Looking back on my life, it is so very clear how true this is: What we focus our energy and attention on become the dominant experiences in our lives, good or bad.

Think back to your own life. Can you recall a time when your attention or focus brought something into your life? I have so many examples of this in my life that I could probably write an entire book. I put so much of my energy and attention on having a successful corporate career and got exactly that; I followed my plan without letting anything get in my way. I focused my attention on the next promotion, and the next one, and the next one and, without fail, each one came just as I intended, believed and expected.

The same held true for me with my negative thoughts and attention. I never expected to make the ninth grade girls lacrosse team, but I tried out anyway because that is what all my friends were doing. Although I was devastated when I didn't make the team, I wasn't surprised at all. I knew I wouldn't make it. I can say the same thing about my second failed marriage. Because I already had one bad marriage under my belt, I was convinced that I didn't know how to be a good wife. Not only did I believe that but I also internally wondered about the stability of my marriage and how long it would truly last.

Although I wasn't aware of it at the time, I now know that my thoughts, intentions, beliefs and expectations—my overall mindset— impacted my results. Despite the fact that I wasn't consciously aware of it happening, it's now clear that the power of my thoughts created my experiences and my results.

The saying, "You get what you expect, whether you want it or not," continues to be true in my life. That is why positive expectations, beliefs and optimism are essential to all of us as we let go of the status quo and redefine who we are meant to be.

There are aspects about the power behind our mindsets that are likely familiar to all of us. Visualization—creating pictures in your mind of how you want an event or situation to play out—is a commonly used technique among athletes to help predict their future performance. Pro golfers visualize their shots and Olympic swimmers visualize their strokes or standing on the podium with their medals. Visualization is a powerful mindset shifting and setting technique.

In fact, I was talking about visualization while facilitating a workshop with some clients and there was a brain scientist in the group. She told us that studies on visualization have shown that it reprograms the neural circuitry of the brain, meaning that when you visualize success, your brain is *programmed* to believe the event is successfully happening in that moment. This then sets you up for future success when you actually are in the situation you've visualized.

Once I began to live my life from this new yet familiar knowledge that my thoughts and beliefs create my life, visualization became one of my many common practices. For me, visualizing is more than just seeing, it's writing. In fact, I typically write first before the image becomes clear enough to visualize.

My favorite example of the power of thoughts and their impact is how I met Matt. Months before we met, I contemplated what the perfect relationship would mean for me, and the characteristics of the person with whom I could have that type of relationship. I wrote down every last detail, not quite sure that this person truly existed, however it was fun to pretend he did. Many months after I met him, I rediscovered the list and realized that person did exist, right down to his blue eyes. I remember I didn't want to include too many physical characteristics because, honestly, did it matter what color his hair was? But I am a sucker for blue eyes so decided I'd be quite happy having a set to look into on a regular basis. It was the last item on the list, sort of an afterthought or a "nice to have but not necessary" addition.

Matt was physical evidence that practiced, focused, and positive thought can yield positive results. It happens whether you know it or not (as evident with my prior examples) but it is so incredibly liberating and satisfying to experience that yes, if you believe and focus your energy on something, the Universe will deliver.

Even though I know it is true, living from this perspective takes practice. It's like training your brain to get in shape, just as you would train your body. I had more than twenty-five conscious years of what I call, "living by default" before I realized that I don't have to be a victim of circumstances that surround me. I can adopt a mindset that creates life experiences.

Does this mean I ignore what's going on around me? No, because what I do is choose how to interpret what is going on in my environment. I'm also selective about whom I surround myself with.

When I first established my business, I had to tune out the negative chatter about the recession, how many small businesses fail in the first three years, how hard it is to start a business and how much harder it is to keep a successful one going. Those sentiments were based on other people's journeys and experiences, not mine. I knew I could have easily bought into all of that but I also knew and had proven that I would get what I expected and believed, so I refused to accept any of those "facts." Was it easy? No, especially when, as I mentioned earlier, I had one of my biggest supporters (my mom) continually reminding me how hard it was to start a business. It was essential for me to have thoughts that created beliefs and expectations of a successful, profitable business. That was essential for me to get past the fear of being in that percentage of small businesses that fail. As mentioned before, a belief is simply a thought we keep thinking, so if you want to change your beliefs, change your thoughts and keep changing them until they become your inherent beliefs.

What are your beliefs about yourself, your life, and whatever area it is you are looking to redesign? Are they supportive of your success or do they need to change? Where did they come from?

Beliefs and expectations are often a result of messages we have heard throughout our lives. They often start with our parents and teachers, and, as I've shared with several examples, then are reinforced by our personal experiences throughout our lives.

For instance, I had beliefs that weren't supporting me—beliefs about what it meant to be in a successful relationship and about my own ability to be a good wife or partner. Just as with starting my own business, I knew for my personal life to be a success on all fronts, I needed to shift my mindset before my results would shift. I spent (and continue to spend) time learning from the many masters, such as Deepak Chopra, Wayne Dyer, Marianne Williamson and Tony Robbins, about using the power of positive mindset to create positive life experiences.

For me it is a daily practice. Just like keeping my body in shape by running and working out on a regular basis, I have to work on my mindset. I had over twenty-five years of not paying much attention to where my thoughts were focused but instead living with the results of where they were focused. I've learned to choose a more deliberate approach, and, if I'm not experiencing what I want in my life, I look internally to see what needs to shift so that the external results will then follow.

The other piece of mindset that plays an important role is the amount of personal responsibility we take for the results we experience. If I see outcomes in my external environment that are not to my liking, I take responsibility. I never used to do that. Before, I would just get mad at whoever or whatever was in my way. Now I know better. I used to blame other people or circumstances, but now I look at what *I* can change to get different results. I know that I am responsible for all results and outcomes that surround me because I choose my reactions. I cannot control what others do or say, or what

they think of me and what I'm doing; I can only choose how I react to what occurs around me.

Knowing this creates a sense of control in a world in which many things are uncontrollable. I can always control how I react and what I do in response to what goes on around me. Having this knowledge has an overall impact on my mindset about my ability to create more and more positive experiences in my life. Why? Because I choose how I look at the experience and I can always choose to find the good in what may appear to be bad.

I use this approach when I bid on contracts for my business. If I desire to win a contract and expect to win, I will take personal responsibility and do what is required to support that outcome. I do all that it takes so that I am confident enough with the proposal, one that I feel best supports what the client needs. And if by chance my company doesn't win, I take personal responsibility for the loss. I don't blame it on the competition, the potential client, or their small budget, but instead recognize that we could have done something differently and seek the lessons to be learned for the next opportunity. Of course I get disappointed if we don't win a contract but I choose to find the lesson as opposed to allowing my thoughts to become overly negative.

Just as I heard in my high school gym when I was fourteen years old, how we view our day and what happens in it is our choice. Taking responsibility for your mindset and the results you see in your life is also a choice. When you make that choice, you are completely in the driver's seat.

Deciding you want to shift your mindset and perspective is also a choice. It takes making a decision and then acting on it. It means inspecting your beliefs and expectations and deciding, first, where they came from, and second, if they are serving you. After you make the choice to shift your mindset, you must practice, just as you would when learning any new skill.

That's what it was like for me. It was about learning a new way of thinking about life, about myself and about my role in creating the life I wanted. I believe that learning the "new way of thinking" was actually remembering a very old way of thinking. When we are kids we believe we can do anything and live from this place. I remember this from when I was very young—the world of make-believe, pretending to be a doctor or a model or an actress, was very real to me.

My ten-year-old niece has told me more than once that she knows and believes she can be and do anything. I overheard her tell Debra she could be anything she wanted as long as she believed. She said, "Mama, you just have to think you can do it and you will." I am certain I had the same inherent knowledge when I was young. We are born with it and then, as we get older, we begin to internalize the messages and beliefs of our parents, teachers, friends and society, eroding our internal optimism and mindset. It is up to us to recognize that and reclaim what we have always known—our mindset can be a powerful asset.

On my journey of reinvention (which still continues) I learned (or perhaps relearned) that not only are positive beliefs and an optimistic mindset crucial for a successful life redesign or transformation, but also are essentially the foundation of all successful outcomes. You must believe in your own ability to get where you want to go and expect only the positive results you desire for your dreams to become your reality.

Your mindset consists of your thoughts, intentions, expectations, and beliefs. All of them determine your results. How big can you dream? You can be anything you want and can create your life to be exactly as you want it to be, as long as you believe in yourself and your ability to get there. You create the capacity and capability by shifting your

mindset to support your desires, as in *The Wizard of Oz* when Glenda the Good Witch said to Dorothy, "You always had the power."

One of my favorite quotes by Marianne Williamson sums up how powerful our thoughts and beliefs about ourselves are in creating the life we desire:

> *Our deepest fear is not that we are inadequate. Our deepest fear is that we are powerful beyond measure. It is our light, not our darkness that most frightens us. We ask ourselves, Who am I to be brilliant, gorgeous, talented, fabulous? Actually, who are you not to be?*

Believe in your brilliance, your talents, your fabulousness, and your light. You have the power—just believe.

Julie's Story

STAYING POSITIVE

Promise me you'll always remember you're braver than you believe, you are stronger than you seem, and smarter than you think. —Winnie the Pooh

Winnie the Pooh has a diverse tribe and I truly applaud him for embracing what each member brings with their own uniqueness. Are you a Tigger or are you an Eeyore? Quick, without thinking too much, which are you more like? Do you wake up ready to get the day started? Are you eager to find out what new experience life offers you every day? Tigger certainly embraces life to the fullest. He literally bounces through his days. Where does he find the energy to be so enthusiastic? Does he wake up every single day with the positive attitude? Or does he simply choose to be happy?

Believe it or not, I've actually considered Tigger's approach to life on more than one occasion. Along my journey I've used him as a personal attitude role model to get me out of bed. And I'm not too proud to admit it has worked.

Do you actively manage your personal outlook and attitude? Your thoughts, beliefs and expectations define the life you will live. I've seen examples of this over and over again. Countless friends and acquaintances have shared stories of the power of positive thinking. Deepak Chopra and Anthony Robbins have changed lives through sharing their secrets about positive thinking. Throughout my own journey it has been proven to me over and over again.

When I found myself unemployed, it was a pivotal moment in my life. I was at a crossroads and didn't know what was around the bend. Although I couldn't control much about the situation, I was able to make a conscious decision to have a positive mindset. I knew the only thing I could control was how I reacted to what life was throwing at me. Goodness knows I had plenty of reasons to hole up in the house for weeks eating chocolate and wallowing in the abyss. That wasn't my style. The only way I knew how to get through this challenging situation was to simply get through it. I didn't allow myself to give any energy to the negative thoughts.

Goal-setting was the singular way I managed the journey of reinventing myself professionally. It was incredibly important for me to set daily goals. I was terrified of the unknown—I imagine this is a feeling you've had on your journey—and I did my best to manage outside my comfort zone.

For me, setting a goal for the day or a few goals for the week was my way of gaining a glimpse of my former life. It provided me with a means to transition into the reinvention process while still giving me confidence in my former self. Let's be honest, I wasn't going to reinvent myself in one day. Micro-goals were the key to getting me through the more difficult times.

One day the goal was to attend an 8:00 a.m. networking session. Anyone familiar with the DC area traffic can appreciate the challenge of getting to a networking event at that hour. It wasn't easy to walk into a room of strangers and acknowledge I was unemployed. I was terrified of what they would think. Would they immediately think being laid off was code for something else? Would they assume all the talented HR professionals are employed so there must be something wrong with me? How would I respond when someone asked, "Where are you working?" My personal identity was so closely tied to my professional identity I literally had a panic attack trying to anticipate how I would answer these questions.

In spite of the lingering doubt in my mind, I pulled into the parking garage at 7:45 a.m. and took a deep breath. I reminded myself of my own strength, courage and skill. I entered the room and began to scan the crowd for a familiar face. Within ten minutes I saw three people with whom I was comfortable sharing my unique situation. I was met with empathy, compassion and support when I was able to be vulnerable and honest. I was humbled by their kindness. A former graduate school professor volunteered to introduce me to a potential client. SCORE! As I drove away, I remember thinking how grateful I was that I had taken the risk to go to this event. What if I hadn't acted with courage and conviction and put myself out there? I would have missed this amazing opportunity, and, more important, missed the chance to benefit from the kindness of others when I needed it most.

As my journey as an "unexpected entrepreneur" continued, I had my fair share of days when I craved time with caring, nurturing people. Going from a team of people to a one-woman operation took a high degree of adaptability. In the hours when I came face to face with self-doubt it was refreshing to be able to rely on my tribe to remind me I was going to survive this challenging time. The support I received from my tribe allowed me to stare down the self-doubt. I was able to keep a positive mental attitude and take one step at a time thanks to my men and women who had my back.

I continually make an active decision to remain positive and expect the best. Often on my entrepreneurial journey I don't know what is around the next turn. Sometimes I don't even see the turn coming. I love the challenge of serving my clients and growing my business, however it isn't always rainbows and sunshine. The challenge of business development and serving clients is a constant, positive tension in my life. I don't know from month to month how I will get

new clients. There have been times when I have found myself with available time and no clients. It is easy at these times to get dragged back down into the negative space. I've learned to allow myself a short amount of time to feel the raw emotions at that moment. Once I acknowledge the fear, I channel it into motivation.

While I can't tell you who will be my next client, I can say with confidence there *will* be a new client. Staying positive in uncertain situations allows me to harness the power of stress and turn it into something positive. Whether it is asking current clients for referrals or speaking at a workshop, I find the positive energy propels me much farther than the negative. Tigger continues to serve as my role model as my journey continues.

THE ROAD TO MOTHERHOOD

Remaining positive about your job is one thing, but maintaining a positive outlook about my journey to motherhood took more than even I knew I was capable of. One of the many unexpected turns my journey of letting go of the status quo has provided is the opportunity to share my unique story.

One thing I needed to reconcile when I began to write this book was letting go of the intense secrecy I've held about my path to becoming a mom. I wasn't entirely comfortable putting the intimate details of my life on paper. I knew I wanted this book to serve as inspiration to other women who were in need of affirmation and positive reinforcement. I grew stronger from others while I was on my journey to motherhood and it is my sincere hope that by sharing my conception story it will serve as a source of inspiration and strength for women who may also be struggling with infertility.

In late September of 2010 Greg and I celebrated our ninth wedding anniversary. We clearly saw our future with children. Losing the pregnancy in August of 2010 strengthened our resolve to have a child. After eighteen months without getting pregnant, we knew something had to change in order for us to have a child. For whatever reason we were both reluctant to seek medical assistance. I felt like I was admitting I was a failure. Why did I need help getting pregnant when I saw countless people conceiving without even trying? There were reality shows about unintended pregnancies and women who didn't even *know* they were pregnant. Yet I was terribly nervous about seeking medical help. It felt like something I should be able to accomplish alone. As a high achiever my whole life I felt like a personal failure, as a wife and a woman. After much conversation, lots of tears and contemplation, Greg and I finally agreed to take it one step at a time. We reconciled ourselves to the fact that we were comfortable seeking assistance in conceiving a child. Part of the process of letting go of the status quo for me was admitting it was perfectly acceptable to ask for help. There was no shame in getting assistance to achieve the dream of parenthood. I hope in my lifetime I can see an end to the social stigma that surrounds infertility and seeking reproductive assistance.

On a beautiful October day we found ourselves in the office of a fertility specialist. Never in my wildest dreams did I think there would be anyone else besides my husband and me involved in conceiving a child. I spent my entire adult life trying not to get pregnant and here we were at a fertility specialist, discussing options with a wonderfully caring and supportive specialist. We were able to get pregnant in July of 2010 without medical assistance, which the doctor acknowledged as positive. He was optimistic we could conceive by using intrauterine insemination (IUI). IUI is a procedure that involves placing sperm inside a woman's uterus to facilitate fertilization. As with any reproductive health matter, it isn't a slam-dunk one-size-fits-all solution.

We had to decide how aggressive we wanted to be with this process. IUI was the least invasive option but it also had the lowest success rate. Since we were able to get pregnant three months earlier, we hoped that with limited assistance we could get pregnant again. We ultimately decided to take the less aggressive option and proceed with IUI.

In a matter of days I found myself dealing with a team of people from nurses to doctors and pharmacists helping us with our dream to start a family. What happened to a fun night at a bar followed by some crazy sex? When did it get so difficult to have a baby? Why was it going to take twenty healthcare professionals to help us become parents? I remember thinking, *Normal people don't go to these lengths to have a child. Maybe the Universe is telling me I shouldn't be a parent. Maybe I am too selfish to be a good mom. Only three months earlier my body literally rejected being pregnant. Who do I think I am to control the Universe this way?* These were the tapes playing in my head as we navigated through the journey to conception.

I continued to push aside the ideal visions I had about how I would become a mother. I reconciled the options that were presented to me. Before long I began to embrace how fortunate I was to have access to healthcare professionals who could make our dreams a reality. By allowing myself to acknowledge my previous vision of motherhood, mourn the loss of our first child and embrace the support we found in our medical team, I was able to shift my entire outlook on how my family would develop. Our goal was to have a healthy child and the end result was what mattered. Letting go of my unattainable dreams and embracing the reality was instrumental in my journey to motherhood.

We began our protocol to attempt IUI on October 1, 2010. After successfully learning how to inject the necessary drugs, we were cautiously optimistic. IUI involves strict protocols with follow-up appointments and constant monitoring of levels and indications to ensure ideal timing for attempted conception. I was learning more about conception than I ever wanted to know!

After the final test to determine the feasibility of continuing with the protocols, we learned things weren't progressing as expected. Our doctor usually preferred to see a significantly higher number on one of the tests and we were only at 30 percent of the goal. I was devastated. Yet again we couldn't get a break. What was wrong with me? Rather than see the 30 percent possibility of getting pregnant I was fixated on the less than stellar results. Doubt began to creep back into my mind. Was I denying Greg the chance to be a dad? Was I the reason why we couldn't get pregnant sooner? Why was my body betraying me again?

Fortunately Greg continued to be optimistic and knew we would be parents. He assured me this would happen for us when the timing was right. He was a pillar of strength and confidence. Greg reminded me that we were taking this process step by step and not to get ahead of ourselves. He saw the glass half full and was ready to drink every last drop. Before I knew it I found my outlook changing and saw hope in the situation.

A few days later Greg and I were in the doctor's office for the transfer. What an odd appointment. I wondered how many other people our doctor had assisted with conception. I found him incredibly warm and reassuring. My analogy was a highway with lots of traffic. In order to get to the destination faster we were using the high occupancy vehicle (HOV) lanes. We just needed some assistance getting things to the destination faster. The doctor managed my expectations accordingly. He reiterated our reduced odds, given our previous test results. While I didn't want to be negative about the experience, I attempted to manage my expectations appropriately.

For the next few days I limited my activity and did my best to remain positive. The weeks that followed the transfer seemed to be the longest of my life. The possibility of being pregnant was constantly on my mind. I was so excited, yet I still managed to be fairly guarded given the miscarriage. About the time I was supposed to get my period I remember feeling overwhelmed every single time I would go to the bathroom. *Will I be bleeding? Is this the time I am going to fall apart again? Please don't let me see anything red.*

I remember bargaining with God on several occasions. *Just let me get pregnant again and I promise I'll be a better person. Give me a sign things will be okay. I promise I can take care of this baby better than the last one. Trust me!*

The idyllic vision I had of making a wonderful dinner and presenting Greg with baby booties on a platter was simply not the reality I was living. We would learn our fate through a blood test. It occurred to me several strangers would know I was pregnant before Greg and I would. Isn't that weird? Isn't this supposed to be a special moment between Greg and me? Again, I revised my visions of how we would find out we were pregnant because our path was unique to us. Our path was lined with many supportive people who wanted nothing more than for us to become parents. It certainly didn't hurt that our fans were skilled medical professionals.

On a bright, early November morning I found myself back in the doctor's office. Fortunately for patients in my situation, the turnaround time for blood work is mercifully quick. The upside is you know the news quickly—the downside is the news isn't always good. How do you book your day around a four-hour window that could be the best or worst news of your life? Walking out of the doctor's office I was proud of the courage we summoned even to get to this point in our parenthood journey. I took solace knowing the information we would receive in the next few hours would be better than having taken no action at all.

Nothing prepares you for the moment you see the doctor's office number pop up on your cell phone. My heart literally skipped a beat when I saw it. I knew this call would change my life, one way or another. As I prepared myself for the news, I kept hearing Greg's words of encouragement in my ear: "We will take this one step at a time." The kind nurse who only three months earlier told me my levels were falling had the privilege of telling me we were, in fact, pregnant.

Tears filled my eyes. We made it! We actually got pregnant! Finally, we were presented with the chance to be parents, again. The nurse said she wanted to have me come back in three days to confirm my levels were rising. As I hung up the phone I relished in the pure magic of knowing I was going to be a mother. I knew this pregnancy would be different. I had a positive outlook and was going to do everything within my power to nurture and grow this baby.

The power of remaining positive is essential to your journey of reinvention. Without keeping a positive attitude, you won't have the energy to continue on your journey when dark moments strike. By never even acknowledging the negative thoughts and self-talk, you eliminate obstacles from your path before they materialize. I knew finding my ideal job was possible and remained positive about the prospect of taking my career to the next level. I simply didn't expect it to occur at the same time I was going to start a family. These two things coinciding weren't in my plan, however I found myself in this very place and my positive attitude became increasingly more important day by day.

Think about the Eeyores you know. They always seem to have a dark cloud above them wherever they go. You ask them how they are doing and undoubtedly the stories they share are negative. We all have challenges in our lives. We can't control what happens to us, we can only control how we react. You can make a conscious choice to react positively or negatively to life. The choice is yours and yours alone.

You Get What You Expect
Whether You Want It or Not

Your mind is incredibly powerful. You ultimately decide what is going to have power and influence over your life. You can determine and define what you read, watch and listen to and who you interact with each and every day. Are you making choices out of habit? Obligation? Self-interest? Self-preservation? Give some thought to the most influential aspects of your life. Are they adding to your joy or sucking your energy? You can create the life you want, however it may not be an easy journey. Allow yourself to be worthy of authentic happiness. Give yourself permission to acknowledge the past, change the present and alter your future for the better.

Remember:

- Your mindset is your most powerful tool to create the life you want.

- Examine your beliefs about your life. Where did they originate? Are they serving you?

- Take small steps to start shifting your beliefs and expectations to those that serve you. This takes coming from the "observer" mode and monitoring your thoughts and feelings.

- Take personal responsibility for the results and experiences in your life. If you don't like what you see externally, examine how you can shift something internally to have a new perspective or a better view of the situation.

- Remember you cannot control what goes on around you but you can control your reactions and how you view what occurs. You can always reframe past events in the light of how they served you and the positive lessons you learned from them.

- You have the power to create your life by design. Believe in your brilliance and know you deserve all you desire.

Ask Yourself:

- Am I a Tigger or an Eeyore?

- What do I surround myself with regularly?

- What is my first reaction to bad news?

- Who are the most influential people in my life? Are they optimistic? What can I learn from them?

- Are there Eeyores in my life? Should I distance myself from them?

CHAPTER 7:
WHO ARE YOU TALKING TO
AND WHAT ARE YOU SAYING?

The most important conversations you will ever have are those that go on inside your own head. Your internal dialogue and chatter can and will impact the actions you take and the results you get in all areas of your life. This element is about paying attention to your self-talk and taking action to ensure you are speaking to yourself as you would your best friend or daughter. As you move along your journey, being kind to yourself is of the utmost importance. Being your own biggest supporter and treating yourself with the highest regard will ease your journey and keep your confidence strong. Learning to love yourself is integral to your journey and it begins with your inner voice. You want to take care of and treat yourself as you do those you love; this starts with the conversations going on inside your head . . . who are you talking to and what are you saying? Learning to change the internal soundtracks from negative ones to those that support the woman and the life you are creating will be one of the most rewarding parts of your journey.

—Julie & Andria

Andria's Story

You must love yourself before you love another. By accepting yourself and fully being what you are, your simple presence can make others happy.
—Author Unknown

You, yourself, as much as anybody in the entire universe, deserve your love and affection. —Buddha

NO ONE CAN LOVE YOU MORE THAN YOU LOVE YOURSELF

Do you love yourself?

I'm serious. Do you?

You may be thinking, "Of course I do!" But do you really?

I can ask this question three times because I, too, would typically respond, "OF COURSE!" when asked if I loved myself; yet when I really started to investigate whether or not that was true, my actions spoke much louder. Maybe I didn't love myself as much as I thought I did.

I heard a statistic that adults have approximately 60,000 to 80,000 thoughts a day. That's crazy, isn't it? What would happen if you started to pay attention to even one-third of those 60,000 thoughts? For one-third of your waking hours, try to listen to the internal dialogue running through your mind. What is the soundtrack playing in your head? And of that one-third of the time that you're paying attention to your internal dialogue, what percentage of that is actual

self-talk? You know, the talk that begins when you wake up in the morning and look in the mirror. What do you say? *"Good morning beautiful, you look ravishing today! Let's make it another fantastic day!"*? Or is it more like what used to run through my head as I squinted my eyes to adjust to the bathroom light and thought to myself, *Oh Andria, you look so tired. You need to get rid of the luggage under your eyes. Where did THAT wrinkle come from? I swear it wasn't there yesterday. I think we need to get better lighting in here. You look awful.* And then I'd brush my teeth and get on with my day without thinking anything was wrong with what just occurred.

We are so self-critical, aren't we? Think about it. Think of the things you say to yourself, and ask yourself if you would EVER say anything like that to the female child in your life, whether it's your daughter, granddaughter, niece, or little sister. Would you EVER look at her and tell her she looks awful and perhaps she needs to stand under better light? I cringe when I think of anyone saying anything of the sort to my ten-year-old niece. I'd probably smack them if they ever talked to her that way. Yet I had no problem talking to myself this way. Why is that? Why is it okay to berate ourselves? Is it because no one can hear us? What would you think if you knew everyone could hear you? What if there was an internal microphone that broadcast all your internal chatter out in public? Would you be proud or embarrassed?

I am happy to say that today I'd be proud about 60 percent of the time and the other 40 percent would be embarrassing. For me, getting to that 60 percent positive self-talk has been a huge accomplishment considering that until about six years ago I had a 95 to 5 ratio of negative to positive self-talk. So getting to 60/40 is huge!

If I think back to how my internal dialogue started, I have to go back to when I was a kid. After all, I was pretty much a blank slate, as we all are, when I came into this world. I grew up around some self-critical people and began picking up some of their habits. I don't blame it on anyone. I just internalized some bad habits while at the same time placing high expectations on myself. I have always set a very high bar for myself and if I didn't reach it, I was very hard on myself.

I always got good grades in school so if I brought home the occasional low grade on a test, my parents knew it was a fluke. They never gave me a hard time. It was simply, "Do better next time." Yet I was the one saying to myself (in the harshest of tones) *What's wrong with you, Andria? Why didn't you do better?* **I was angry with myself for not doing better and not being "good enough." Good enough for what? Who knows, but there was definitely that feeling of "I must do more to get better." As I write this, I realize it has been a common and almost never-ending tape in my head that I must do more and more to get better and better and to reach my goals. I was always pushing myself in this way.**

My family moved a few times in the first twelve years of my life because my dad was transferred for his job. During these times, I experienced a recurring sense of insecurity about entering new schools. It's never fun being the new kid in the class and I put a lot of pressure on myself to make friends quickly. Because I was so selective about who I wanted to "let in" to my personal space, making friends wasn't easy, and the internal dialogue running in my head was harsh. I also compared myself to Debra, who made friends very easily. So there was a lot of negative chatter that started when I was young. I was self-critical regarding friends, how long it took me to get comfortable in every new town and new school, and, of course, when I wasn't getting the best grades. The older I got, the harsher I was with myself.

After my first marriage ended, I went to see a counselor. I was twenty-five years old and it was the first time anyone ever asked me the question: "Do you love yourself?" I saw the most wonderful therapist on and off for several years and she really helped me begin to understand what self-love was all about (although it took me much longer to begin to practice it). I thought it was narcissistic.

After all, I grew up with the message that women were to be selfless. We were to give everything to everyone around us because that was the "right thing to do," regardless of the fact that we might end up depleted until the kids left home and we had "time" to take care of ourselves. That is not self-love, and true self-love is not narcissistic. It means taking care of yourself, nurturing yourself and treating yourself as you would your very best friend, your daughter, your niece or your little sister. Love of self sets you up for huge success in your life. When you can express your own self-love, you are even more able to express it to others. It's meant to set you up for huge rewards and a life filled with love.

When my therapist asked me if I truly loved myself, I said, "Of course I do!" But upon further exploration it became obvious that despite the fact that I thought I loved myself, I didn't treat myself with the respect and kindness I deserved. This became more and more obvious to me as I found myself in my second unhappy marriage. I told myself over and over again that how I felt was irrelevant. I used words and phrases like *Stop it, Andria. Get over it. You're fine. You have a good life. Don't be so picky. Don't be so ungrateful.* What would I have said to my niece (who at that time was under the age of five!)? Certainly not "Stop it, Nicole. Get over it. You'll be fine—don't be ungrateful." No. Instead I would have told her, "Honor your feelings, follow your heart, and get on with it. For that, you will be eternally grateful."

I actually did ask myself that question in the midst of my turmoil at that time in my life: *What if it were twenty-five years from now and Nicole came to you to tell you she is feeling all the things you're feeling right now? What would you tell her?* There was never a hesitation in my response. I knew I would tell her the opposite of what I told myself. So why couldn't I tell myself to honor myself and get on with it? Why couldn't I show myself the same level of respect I'd give my niece? Deep down I'm not sure I believed I deserved to feel much better or have anything better. After all, I was gauging my life on what other people defined as success. I looked at my life and it looked pretty damn good to the outsider, and that is what kept me stuck. I was telling myself, in a very abrasive manner, NOT to listen to my heart, that something was "wrong with me" because I was unhappy. I was telling myself I wasn't being grateful for my current life because I wanted to make some big changes. Yes, my negative self-talk worked its magic and kept me firmly cemented in place.

Self-talk is very powerful. It's what we hear constantly, and unless you are good at quieting your mind, it can be hard to escape the chatter. My negative self-talk prevented me from doing what a person who loved me would tell me to do. It was a powerful force in my life but it took me years to recognize that it had any impact on me at all. Once I recognized the force of negative self-talk, I learned that positive self-talk could be just as powerful, if not more so, although it takes retraining of the brain (a lot of retraining in my case!). It requires attention to what you're thinking and feeling so you can record over the negativity. Although I was first asked about whether I loved myself when I was twenty-five, it took me ten more years before I consciously started treating myself with the love and respect I deserved. It was during my moments of silence, when I started creating space in my life to hear important messages, that I also heard my internal critic speaking quite loudly to me.

As I began to understand how powerful our thoughts are in creating what we experience, I wanted to change a lot of my internal dialogue. It's not easy to monitor all that chatter but what makes it easier is paying attention to how you feel. Your feelings are an indicator of what you are thinking. So clearly, if I am berating myself for something, I don't feel very good. Recognizing these bad feelings would cause me to stop and pay attention to what thoughts were going through my head at that moment. That is usually when I identified the negative thought creating the negative feelings and that's when there was an opportunity to make a change.

Awareness is just the first step. Actually changing the dialogue and self-talk takes practice and effort. I wanted to make a change because I was acutely aware of the impact the negative self-talk had on me throughout most of my life. It held me back, created fear and anxiety, and it made me feel bad. That was not what I wanted to experience anymore.

While living on my own after my divorce, I spent time focused on myself and reclaiming my own identity. This was specific time to nurture myself and was when I started to transform myself into a more self-loving person. What did I do? I created positive affirmations about Andria. Yes, I made lists of the things I loved about myself and affirmed those things aloud. I asked my trusted friends and family members what they loved about me.

I put signs on my bathroom mirror and on my refrigerator—sticky notes that said, "I love you," "You are fabulous," "Good morning, Beautiful." At first it felt awkward and then it was funny because I certainly didn't feel beautiful at 5:00 a.m. staring at my face in the bathroom mirror.

However, eventually, it became a habit. And when it became internalized like a habit, I knew my dialogue had shifted. Another gauge that helped tremendously was the question I asked myself about what I would say to Nicole. Asking myself this question always brought me back to being a loving person. I pushed myself to treat me as I would treat Nicole. It continues to be a wonderful indicator of the amount of love and respect I give myself.

Another gauge I use is asking myself, *What if my public internal microphone were turned on right now?* This continues to work very well for me, especially because I need these types of barometers to remind me to get back to a self-loving place. Due to years of habitual behavior, it's easy for me to slip back into self-criticism.

One recent, busy day, while running around to various client appointments, I ended up getting stuck on an extremely crowded platform of one of the DC metro lines. There was a problem with the train line that day and I ended up in the thick of it. Standing there waiting for the next train with hundreds of other people, not knowing when the next train would arrive, I got anxious that I would be late for my next appointment. I started to scold myself for getting in this situation, asking, *Why do you always do this to yourself? Cram your schedule and then get stuck in shit like this? You know this city is way OVERCROWDED and you try to do too many things in one day. Why can't you just chill out and spread your appointments out? Now you're all stressed and in this mess.*

And then it hit me. What if my internal microphone turned on at that moment? I laughed to myself at the thought of hundreds of people in the train station hearing the scolding going on inside my head. I was literally yelling at myself. If this were broadcast over a public speaker, they'd be thinking, "Who is the psycho woman yelling like that?" Yes, that put me right back into place. *And what would I say to Nicole if she were in this situation?* I told myself exactly what I would say to her: "It's not a big deal. This stuff happens. People understand. You'll get to your next appointment when you get there. Just relax and breathe." That is what a loving person says to someone they love. And that is what I ended up saying to myself on the train platform that day. It took me a few minutes to get there, and I got there in a roundabout way, but at least I got there.

146

I believe that how you treat yourself is how you teach others to treat you. As women, we can be very hard on ourselves when we should be treating ourselves with only the utmost love and respect. We also won't truly experience love from another until we can love ourselves. For me, being so critical of myself made it okay for others to be critical of me. After all, no one was ever as hard on me as I was on myself, so it never seemed so bad if others weren't treating me well. The truth is we all deserve respect from everyone we encounter; however, if we cannot give it to ourselves, we probably cannot even recognize it from others. That is what I mean when I say that how you treat yourself is how you teach others to treat you. If you aren't nice to yourself, it's okay for others not to be nice to you. Once you begin to love and respect yourself, you teach others to treat you that way. It's the energy you emit and is therefore the energy that comes back to you.

Treating yourself with respect is also about nurturing yourself. This means different things to each of us but it is about taking care of you.

What do you do to take care of yourself? If you had an entire day to yourself, what would you do? How would you spend your time?

This is "you" time. It's all about you and only about you. When you begin to take time for yourself, to honor yourself, you are treating yourself with love and respect. Taking these types of actions also helps shift your internal dialogue. You deserve only the best. Treat yourself this way for this simple but most important reason: You deserve it. When you start loving and respecting yourself like you love and respect your daughter or your niece or your little sister, you will automatically begin to record over the negative tapes playing in your head with the loving feelings that result from nurturing yourself.

As you continue on your journey of re-creating and redesigning your life, as you let go of the status quo, positive self-talk and nurturing is very important. Why? Because you may hear negative messages, you may hear naysayers, and you will likely hear critics on the outside. You want to remember that what's most important is always what's occurring on the inside. Not everyone will love you and what you're doing. Some will be jealous and others will not understand. Through it all you must continue to be kind to yourself, nurture yourself, and love yourself to pieces. It will not only help you ignore what the peanut gallery says, but will also help you recognize that at the end of the day, the most important love in your life is your love for yourself.

Julie's Story

THOUGHTS BECOME BELIEFS, BELIEFS BECOME YOUR TRUTH

Be yourself; everyone else is taken. —Oscar Wilde

What are the conversations you have with yourself on a daily basis? What are the playlists playing in your head? What is on constant repeat in your brain? Can you even identify what is being said over and over? It took me a long time to realize I could change the discussion, that I had the power to change my internal monologue and that I didn't have to continue to hear the same things over and over again.

As the second-born daughter, I took the opportunity to push the envelope of independence early with my parents. I was a natural extrovert and found my dry sense of humor early in life. I thank my mother for giving me the amazing gift of humor.

My family wasn't unique. We were a conventional family with two parents and two children, each with a role to play in the family dynamic. Growing up, Kristi was labeled the "smart daughter" and I was the "funny daughter." I didn't realize how significant these labels were until college. In my late teens I realized that Kristi is actually pretty funny. She has a terrific sense of humor. And, much to my surprise, I am intelligent. I grew up unaware of how significantly these labels shaped my perspective. As an adult I know I have the ability to change my labels. I appreciate the fact that I was encouraged to develop and grow into who I wanted to be regardless of how I was labeled as a child. You, too, can change your labels!

The playlists you hear in your head shape the life you live, consciously or subconsciously. You may not realize how significant these self-dialogues are in your life yet, however I encourage you to reflect on what you're saying to yourself daily. "I look fat in this outfit." "I need to settle down and get married." "I should have another child because all my friends have three kids." "But he makes a good living and he doesn't hit me so I should stay with him. I can't be a single mother."

What tapes are running through your head? How do they impact your actions? What would you do if you didn't have these messages influencing your thoughts?

When we decided to do IUI, I surrendered control and admitted we needed help creating our family. I needed to relinquish the vision I had for getting pregnant and embrace the reality of our journey. When I accepted the idea we weren't successful conceiving on our own, I changed the tapes playing in my head. I went from unsuccessful woman trying to conceive to potentially expectant mother overnight.

When we found out we were pregnant for the second time, I only allowed positive thoughts to enter my mind. I saw myself eight months pregnant. I visualized a newborn baby in my arms. Yes, there were doubts and concerns. Rather than let myself be consumed with the endless number of things that could go wrong with this pregnancy, I did my best to combat the negative thoughts and focused on the positive. This pregnancy would be different. By reprogramming the monologue in my head, I embraced my own power and changed the story.

Exercise is my way of nurturing myself. My perfect day starts with an hour of exercise. Nurturing myself involves reflecting while running or taking a spin class. Truly pushing my physical limits gives me perspective and recharges my batteries. I've learned I'm happier, more productive and enjoy life more when I actively move my body each and every day. During the days following the miscarriage, I allowed myself to truly acknowledge and feel the loss of the baby. Exercise was a way for me to physically expel the sadness I experienced. I also found I needed to take control in some small way and exercising was my ideal medium.

*When was the last time you did something specifically for yourself? Not because you **HAD** to but because you **WANTED** to? What did you do? When a friend calls and needs a favor, do you drop everything to help them? A family member needs you, so you help them out. Why don't you make yourself a priority and nurture yourself? Do you even know what it means to nurture yourself yet?*

It is perfectly acceptable to take the time to understand what it means to nurture your soul. Embrace your individuality and learn what makes you unique!

I've learned that in order to let go of the status quo you need to be able to nurture yourself. Nobody else knows how to recharge your battery except you and nobody is going to make an appointment for you to nurture yourself. Reinventing yourself isn't easy, it isn't fast, and others certainly don't recognize it. The more you invest in nurturing yourself, the better you will feel about yourself.

So give yourself permission to be selfish. Get a pedicure. Go for a walk. Journal for fifteen minutes during lunch. Or better yet, take the afternoon off and play hooky with a friend! Sleep in. Figure out how you'll nurture yourself and make it a priority to do so regularly. Once you get into the habit, it will become second nature. You are worthy of the investment!

Who Are You Talking To and What Are You Saying?

- Pay attention to the internal dialogue running through your mind. Being "conscious" means being able to be in observer mode.

- Recognize when you are being self-critical and make a conscious effort to say kind things to yourself.

- Make a list of all the things you love about yourself. Read through them and state them as affirmations every day.

- As you experience self-criticism, ask yourself, *What words would I use if I were speaking to a child or teen girl in my life?*

- As you experience self-criticism, ask yourself, *Would I be proud or embarrassed if my internal microphone were turned on and this dialogue was broadcast in public?*

- Remember, how you treat yourself is how you teach others to treat you. When you start any kind of new relationship, you are setting new boundaries for how you will be treated. Sometimes we fall back into old patterns and must reestablish what is okay for us. When you respect yourself and your own boundaries, others will, too. When you are kind to yourself, they will be kind to you. So be kind to yourself. You're the only YOU there is.

Ask Yourself:

- How was I nurtured as a child?

- What do I do to nurture myself as an adult? What pleasures and pastimes do I give myself? What do I like to do on my own?

153

- What subjects are my most frequent internal monologues about? Is there a quick phrase I can use to replace these negative messages? (Take a minute to get into the feeling of that new phrase.)

- What do I want my internal monologues to say when my journey is complete?

- What does my reinvented state look like? (Close your eyes and get a clear picture of this and enjoy the feeling state.)

CHAPTER 8:
WHAT'S THE SCORE?

As your journey continues and you are fully in gear moving forward, you may feel the need to "check the score" on how you are doing. How far have you come? How much farther do you have to go? Are you doing this right? This element is all about how "keeping score" can work for you, or not, depending on whose game you're playing and whose rules you're keeping score with. It's about creating your own game, with your own definition of success, from which you can keep your own score, if you want to. It's about letting go of the rules of the games you don't want to be playing and letting go of society's rules and rankings so you can fully step into your own game of life—designed by you. That is the only game you'll ever want to keep score of.

—Julie & Andria

Andria's Story

RUNNING THE RACE WITH YOURSELF

"What's the score?"

"Who's winning?"

"Where do you rank?"

"How did you rate?"

Such common questions, aren't they? It seems that we are always hearing about who is winning the game or what the score is, which company earns the most profit, who ranks highest in this or that. In fact, I believe these common questions and assessments about who is doing something better than someone else have been etched into our brains since we were kids. At least that is how it was for me. Although my parents always told me to do the best I could regardless of what I was doing, there was an underlying drive that not only did I have to do the best, but I also had to be perfect. I was a perfectionist who thrived on getting straight As, on having *at least* a 3.8 GPA while in both college and grad school, and yes, doing the "best I could" because doing that meant I'd be successful. I had the recipe: good grades, good schools, corporate job, success. Check. Check. Check. I was ahead of the game. I was successful. Or was I?

Successful: another word that is etched into my being. What does that mean, really? I know what I learned as a kid and that's what's remained with me for most of my life. Two things about growing up in an Italian family that are forever embedded in my soul are the emphasis on family and, at least in my family, everyone knowing everyone else's business.

For us, family was (and is) the most important thing. I can still hear my Italian grandparents (all four of them) saying, "There's nothing like family!" How close we were as a family and how close you were as an individual with your family members were measures of success (or that was the message I interpreted based on what I saw and heard). Because of this, I was heavily influenced by many of the expectations set for me by family members.

There were clear expectations set forth by my parents (mostly my dad) regarding the type of and level of education I would get. Checked that box. There were also clear expectations set forth less overtly regarding marriage and having children. The subtle messages I picked up as I was growing up were, first, if you weren't married before age thirty, something must be wrong with you, and, second, children were an assumed part of the entire progression of life (after marriage, of course).

Now, keep in mind, these weren't verbalized messages. They were subtle things I picked up on based on how marriage and family were spoken about among my aunts, uncles, cousins, and grandparents. I was okay with the first message about marriage (clearly, since I got married twice) but it was the second one, about children, that I was less certain about. I now think it would have been wise to question both of these messages.

I was never one of those people who had a huge desire to be a mom. Of course, I never wanted to actually admit that, because if you were a member of my family and said something out loud, chances were the rest of the family would know about it by the next day (and this was before email and cell phones). I was afraid that if I admitted that I hated babysitting, my family would think something was wrong with me. I'm sure I believed something was wrong with me, but I hated babysitting and am pretty sure I only babysat twice in my life, at age twelve, for two bratty children and one colicky infant. Those bad experiences didn't scar me because even before I babysat 1 felt uncomfortable around people under the age of ten (except, of course, when I was under the age of ten, and, except today, with my niece and nephew). Yet I was a play-by-the-rules kind of girl, so I knew I'd get married and have kids. Then no one in my family would talk about me.

Kids were always an assumption with my first marriage; however, considering it didn't last long, it never became an issue. In my second marriage, it was talked about but never went further than that. My second husband already had three children, and, again, I just didn't have that burning desire to be a mom—that is, to anything other than animals. The only maternal instinct I ever felt was towards dogs, cats, and pretty much any kind of animal I encountered. Despite how much Debra and I begged our parents to get us a dog or a cat, we never had animals in our home. So ever since I was twenty-two years old, I've had dogs and cats in my life. I am very passionate about adopting animals and definitely pour any maternal energy I have into them.

The older I get the more I realize how programmed I was by societal (and familial) messages about what is right and wrong. Not wanting children seemed "wrong" in so many ways, and not because of anything other than what I heard from other people. Admitting it seemed even more wrong.

When I met Matt, I was almost shocked to discover that he (who had never been married and had no children) also felt this way regarding children. This was a huge relief. Wow, there are other people in their thirties who don't have children, by choice? Child-free by choice, is how we like to phrase it. We are very happy with our decision. We adore our nieces and nephews and are happy to spoil them as much as we can; we are also happy that the only others we share our home with are four-legged creatures. That is how it is today but for many years I was ashamed of the fact that I didn't want children. I was concerned about what other people would think. I was concerned that my family was keeping score and this was one I knew I wouldn't win. And who really likes to lose?

Yet by the time I was thirty-six and getting out of marriage number two, I certainly felt like I was losing in my personal life. And yes, I was keeping score, about everything in my life. I now know the reason I was keeping score was because I assumed everyone else was keeping score, too. I have no idea who "everyone else" was, nor do I really know whose scoreboard I was measuring myself against. It was a scoreboard created from years of programming and making assumptions based on things I heard and observed, not based on what I wanted or needed in my life. By the time I finally realized the only thing I should be assessing myself against is what fulfills and satisfies me, I had years of programming and deep habitual ways of behaving that were not easy to change. I needed to recognize that there wasn't a "success scoreboard" to measure myself against, at least not until I had clearly defined what success meant to me. And even when I did define what success meant to me, was it necessary to keep score?

How do you define success? How much of it is your own definition versus others' definition? By others I mean the people in your life who influence you: your friends and family, teachers, society, and any other people who have impact on your life and your decisions. Having your own definition of success is essential as you go through re-creating or redesigning parts of your life. It's also something that will continue to change as life changes. Priorities change, which means the definition of success will also change.

For me, success meant good grades, advanced education, career, marriage and family, all by (or before) age thirty. Based on that definition, the only things I succeeded at were school and career. Despite the fact that it was not my definition of success, I measured myself against it as if it were the be-all, end-all of my life. As I began to reinvent myself, I had to redefine success from both a personal and professional perspective. Personally, it was extremely difficult because having two failed marriages in my back pocket screamed of failure to me. Pulling success from that meant I had to look in a completely different direction. Success started to become more about how happy I was. This quote from John Lennon defines what I'm talking about: *"When I was five years old, my mother told me that happiness was the key to life. When I went to school they asked me what I wanted to be when I grow up. I wrote down, 'happy.' They told me I didn't understand the assignment. I told them they didn't understand life."*

I almost wish someone had told me this when I was growing up. Happy was never in the equation of what I was told. For all of my adult life my parents have always said that all they want is for me to be happy, but that was not the message I heard growing up. And the messages I did hear, I internalized to a fault—success in one's personal life meant a happy marriage and children. I was twice divorced and didn't want children. For a long time I couldn't get past those facts as meaning anything other than failure. Eventually I looked at it differently and instead of failure, I reframed it to mean that my learned and internalized definition of success (happy marriage and children) was not what success meant for me.

I went on a lot of long runs to figure out what it did mean and could mean, outside of marriage and children. It eventually became about experiencing things that made me happy in my free (non-working) time; that was it. It was simple and I liked it. If a relationship became part of it, fantastic, but if it didn't, I'd still focus on doing things that made me happy in my free time. Doing things that made me happy meant exploring new hobbies, spending time with family and friends, traveling, reading, being with my dogs and cats, and anything else that struck me as fun. From a personal perspective, this continues to define my measure of success today. I am fortunate enough to have met Matt and be in a relationship, which enhances my personal life. Being in a relationship with him has also made me realize that a successful relationship does not necessarily mean marriage. Our relationship's success is based on our terms. Might that include marriage one day? Perhaps, but perhaps not, and either way it's fine because it'll be successful based on our definition of success, not what society or anyone else defines as such.

Professionally, though, redefining success took a slightly different form. Because I was always successful in my career, I knew what worked. Yet starting a business was an entirely new space for me so I wasn't quite sure how to define success. In my personal life, my definition of success seemed to come as a direct result of what hadn't worked for me in the past. Intellectually I knew happiness should play a big part of my description of business success. The reason why we want to achieve anything or reach any goal is almost always because we believe that when we achieve it we will be happier, right? As I built my business, I certainly wanted to be sure I was happy with all aspects of it, yet I wasn't convinced that should be my only measure of success. Hence, I've habitually created metrics against which I evaluate my success—things such as number of clients, total sales, total profits and annual growth. Some of these are vital aspects of running a business and others are aspects that create some anxiety for me.

I continue to ask myself, *Who's keeping score, Andria?* The truth is I'm keeping score and probably the hardest grader of all. However, the longer I am running my business and the older I get, the more I recognize that I'm unwilling to run myself into the ground chasing

161

numbers. At the same time, I know I'm a goal-oriented person so it makes me happy to set personal and professional goals for what I want to achieve, what I want my life to look like (both personally and professionally) and how I want to feel every day when I wake up to start the day. Ensuring that I'm assessing myself against those individually defined goals makes me happy and proud. The challenge is for me to know, without a doubt, that what I'm assessing myself against is truly driven by me and no one else.

Since starting my business, I've had a business coach. I feel privileged to work with and be coached by some very successful business women, yet I have to continue to remind myself that their ideas and suggestions are simply that—ideas and suggestions. They are not instructions or directions. My old habits definitely creep back up: I hear a recipe for success and I instantly want to go implement. It's easy for me to get pulled by what seems to be a perfect blend of information and action for high levels of business success. This type of success means excessive growth, high profits, new clients, etc. I have to consistently pull myself back by asking, "Whose definition of success is this a recipe for?" before I march forward and take action.

Can you relate to this? You start something new in your life and really don't know what success looks like. So you look outside of yourself for the answers. What's she doing? How's she doing it? What process did they follow? And you jump on board thinking that if you follow the same formula, you'll reach your goals. You start to play someone else's game and maybe for a while you're actually winning. Yet eventually you wake up and look around and wonder, as I did, why you're suddenly slipping behind. You feel like you're running 200 mph and falling behind. And then it dawns on you— you're playing a game you don't want to play and tracking your progress against someone else's rules. And yes, that's what I did for most of my life.

I learned that the more I looked externally at what everyone else was saying and doing and assessed myself against that, the easier it was for me to once again fall prey to playing by someone else's rules in someone else's game. I learned to use my gut to determine whether the advice and counsel from coaches and mentors (or family and friends) was the right recipe for me. This is when boundaries come into play and when doing whatever it takes to be successful means more than just marching to someone else's orders. It means doing whatever it takes, per my own marching orders, and assessing my score based on that. For me, this continues to take discipline and practice because I have been practicing different habits, based on others' expectations and definitions, for most of my life.

I've been asked by people I coach and mentor how I keep focus on my goals as my priorities shift. That's the beauty about setting your own goals and tracking yourself against what you define as success: you get to change things anytime you want. Because I like to set and track goals, I'm not one who easily alters them, so it takes a pretty big shift in priorities for me to back off of a goal. But life is not linear and priorities will shift, so we must shift accordingly. The question to ask yourself is "What am I shifting *for*?"

You'll know if it's something important enough to require a change in your direction. You'll also know if it's something that doesn't require any change but is instead a reminder for you to honor your boundaries so you remain on track; because staying focused through shifting priorities is about honoring the boundaries you have set for yourself with respect to your new definition of success. Keep that in mind, and if you're keeping track of how successful you are, ask yourself if the shift in priority will impact your reaching (your definition of) success.

If the answer is yes and you're not comfortable with that, then stay the course, remembering that at the end of the day the only one you must answer to in this area is you. If the answer is yes and you're comfortable with that, then shift your focus accordingly because, again, you must feel satisfied with how you've done against your own definition of success (and yes, you can change it as much as you want to!)

For example, if you have a goal of reaching a certain number of clients and then realize you are spending all your time working with them and no time with your family, you may need to consider shifting to a business model that supports a more balanced life. In this case, you would be shifting for things you want to achieve as part of your definition of success: a higher quality of life and less exhaustion.

As you are going through redesigning any aspect of your life, if you are like me and like to keep track of how you're doing, knowing what you're keeping score against is probably the most important part of this concept. As women, it's so easy to fall into the trap of what we're "supposed" to do and how we're "supposed" to behave, and wait, aren't we supposed to do it all?—be the perfect wife, mother, AND career woman? Try keeping score against that! Seriously, if you think about it, how realistic is it? Something usually falls through the cracks and typically it's the person trying to be that perfect wife, mother and career woman. If that is your definition of success, is it one you created for yourself or one you picked up somewhere along the way? Is an impossible-to-achieve ideal really what you want to assess yourself against?

Some people probably aren't scorekeepers, at least not overtly, and that's perfectly fine. In some fashion, I think we all assess and compare ourselves to others and to the messages we've heard throughout our lives about what it means to be successful. Either way, it's important to assess your own success in a way that works for you. For me, keeping score against another person's definition of winning, or in someone else's game, didn't work. It hindered me because I couldn't win at that game—and I like to win.

Once I got that, I decided to start playing my own game with my own rules. At the same time, as someone who likes to set goals and track myself, I had to find the right thing to track and assess myself against. For me, it's okay to keep score, as long as it's in a game I want to play and it's by my rules. Find what works for you. Create your personal and meaningful definition of success and, if you're a goal tracker, keep score against that and only that. Forget about what everyone else is doing and the games they are playing. Remember, what anyone else thinks of you, your game, your rules, and your life is none of your business.

Julie's Story

If winning isn't everything, then why do they keep score? —_Vince Lombardi_

LIVING YOUR VALUES OUT LOUD

Who won? What's the score? These are questions we ask each and every time we discuss a sporting event. As a child I recall being disappointed with a loss and experiencing the thrill of victory with my youth teams. Today many youth sports teams don't keep score at all. Rather they focus on teaching the fundamentals to children in an effort to develop passionate players, not to beat the competition. To ensure athletes truly understand the fundamentals of a sport it is easier to focus on the _skills_ rather than the final outcome: winning.

What prevents us from applying this same philosophy to our lives? Think about it. Wouldn't it be terrific if you simply were rewarded for learning throughout your life rather than for keeping up with (or beating) the Joneses? Winning would be seen as learning from your mistakes or being true to your authentic self. Imagine the scoreboard being a unique set of criteria tailored to the individual rather than a uniform definition of victory. What a radical concept!

While on my journey, my personal scoreboard changed and evolved as I discovered more about my authentic self. In high school and as a college undergrad, academic success was a primary component of my scoreboard. Clubs and associations and athletics also played a part. As with many freshman women who start college, my weight and physical appearance became something others increasingly evaluated me on. Although it wasn't something I specifically wanted to track, my peers and society told me it was meaningful, so without consciously knowing, I followed the status quo and added my physical

166

appearance to my personal scoreboard. Without even realizing it I was falling victim to what society told me success meant.

It never occurred to me to define success for myself.

In my twenties my scoreboard continued to change. Measuring my self-worth by my pant size was replaced with dazzling my bosses during my internships. Before I knew it, I was looking for my first real job. Gone was the label of where I went to college, and where I _worked_ took its place on the omnipresent scoreboard. It wasn't simply enough to have a real job, soon I found myself feeling pressured to make a certain amount of money. Job title and career progression were the criteria I measured myself with against my peers. Again, who decided what my career success looked like? It certainly didn't feel like I was in charge of this success. Rather, I felt others were telling me what winning in my career looked like and I felt tremendous pressure to achieve _their_ definition of success.

The questions I started asking myself looked like this: _Why am I not able to buy a house yet? What am I doing wrong? Are there higher-paying jobs I should explore? How do I expedite my earning potential? Is graduate school the next move for me?_

I saw friends from college buying condos, new cars, and shopping in the high-end stores every weekend. It seemed like everyone was making great money and experiencing tremendous success. As I continued to refine my personal scoreboard, financial security became increasingly important. I was less concerned with driving the newest model car or having the latest handbag—it was much more important to me to know I could support myself independently. I began to care much less about what others had and simply accepted my authentic self.

Before I knew it I found myself in wedding season. You may be familiar with this stage. All your friends get engaged at once and suddenly you're attending five weddings in one year. You are planning wedding showers and know the ins and outs of the wedding registry better than Ms. Manners herself. Weekends are spent in bridal salons with girlfriends trying to find the perfect wedding dress to represent their individuality. You are carrying the bridal bouquet and train for your girlfriend as she floats down the aisle to her Prince Charming.

The scoreboard at this point for all my friends was turning into who is engaged and who is still single. What is the size of her engagement ring? How many guests is she inviting to the wedding? Where is the happy couple honeymooning and for how long? I was genuinely happy for my girlfriends but found myself nowhere near ready to get married. My scoreboard still contained things like job satisfaction, retirement account balance, number of weeks of vacation, and strong friendships. Talk about letting go of the status quo!

Before I knew it my friends were having children and I wasn't even in a committed relationship. What was wrong with me? I was introduced to everyone's "single friend" who was nice, cute, and had a great job. The problem was I wasn't ready to settle down. I wanted to travel! I couldn't articulate what I wanted in a spouse so how could I possibly be ready to get married? Who said I needed to have my first child by the time I was thirty? Where did it say I couldn't wait to get married until I found the right guy?

What I discovered along the way to defining my life was a strong focus on my personal values and that my scoreboard needed to reflect them. In order to understand what I wanted to track on the success spectrum I needed to have a clear understanding of these values. I would relish opportunities to reflect on what was meaningful and important to me. I jumped at any chance I had to read about personal motivators and beliefs. Throughout my twenties and into my thirties I became acutely aware of what I valued most.

I was truly blessed to find a husband who shared the same core values. Together we were able to articulate our mutual values as well as give each other permission to have unique individual values. We created our scoreboard together and managed to keep our personal scoreboards as well.

Having a clear understanding of our mutual scoreboard and being able to discuss it openly and honestly are critical success factors for our relationship. We both value our careers and financial security so we focused a great deal of our energy on creating and supporting our career growth. Having a financial safety net is something we both needed in order to feel secure. Living without debt is another part of our mutual scoreboard. This requires a level of honesty and transparency that isn't without challenges. However, since it is meaningful to both of us, we are committed it.

One of the most obvious external components of the personal scoreboard is family. I had the good fortune to be a part of raising several children as a part-time nanny during college. I understood firsthand the level of effort it took to raise children. My husband and I had a tremendous amount of freedom and independence, both things we valued highly. Early on in our relationship we decided that parenthood probably wasn't for us.

As I explained earlier, when we would tell people we weren't going to have children, many simply couldn't comprehend. Why wouldn't you have kids? Don't you like children? You'd make such amazing parents! What do you do with your time if you don't have children? While it was fairly progressive to elect not to have children, we weren't trying to make a statement. We felt both of us needed to be fully committed to parenthood before we took the plunge.

169

Therefore, until we were both on the same page at the same time, we would remain child-free by choice. That didn't change the scoreboard others were using to evaluate us, however. Each year after Thanksgiving, the holiday cards would roll into our mailbox filled with photos of sweet families. We'd send our holiday card out, usually a picture of the two of us from a vacation we took that year, and prepare ourselves for the unspoken judgment. At a holiday party we hosted, my husband welcomed our guests with a toast and several of the guests expected him to announce we were pregnant.

It wasn't easy, however I remained true to my authentic self. I knew deep down I was making the right decision for me and trusted my husband would articulate his desires as well. As long as we remained steadfast in our personal beliefs and values, we would make the right decisions. Yes, it is difficult not meeting the milestones society told me I was supposed to achieve. However, it was extremely liberating to know my personal desires and goals were being accomplished. I am a better woman because of the path I chose to take. And ultimately, when Greg and I were both on the same page about having a child, we were as ready as you can be to become parents. Our relationship was tested and strengthened on the path to parenthood, and because we were confident in our beliefs and personal scoreboard, we were able to successfully navigate the path.

Knowing who I am and what I wanted out of life allowed me to create the life I dreamed of without fear and anxiety about what others think. I wasted years desiring what others had (or what I *thought* they had) instead of embracing what I was given. This wasted energy prevented me from any personal growth. I spent an inordinate amount of time and energy trying to achieve what was on other people's scoreboards. I could have spent this time and energy getting to know my authentic self in an effort to fully understand my values and personal motivators.

170

My advice? Invest in yourself! Don't read the ESPN scroll at the bottom of the TV screen. Your score isn't going to show up there, I promise! Set out to quantify how you will measure your success—personally, professionally, spiritually, emotionally, physically.

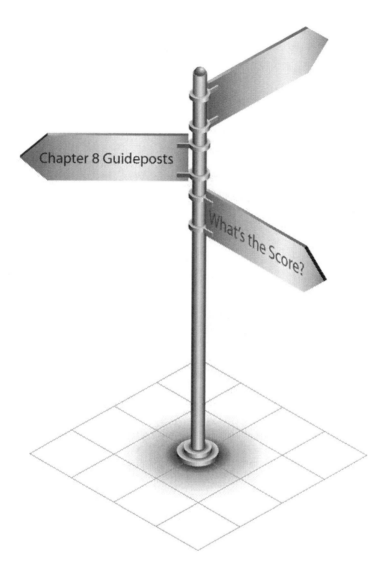

WHAT'S THE SCORE?

Whose rules are you living by and what are these rules?

- Parents: What did they teach you explicitly? What did they teach you by example? Were they happy?

- Teachers/professors: What did they teach you? What was acceptable to them and are you still living based on their acceptance?

- Peers: Are you trying to "keep up" with your peers and comparing your life to theirs?

- Society: How influenced are you by what society deems as the "best" or "right" way to live your life? Where do these societal messages come from and how big a role do they play in the decisions you make?

- Religion: If you were raised in a religious home, how are these messages or beliefs impacting your life today? Are they serving you well? If not, what can you do to change the impact they have on your life?

Did any of these authority figures emphasize putting yourself first and that it's important to be happy? Were you taught that when you're happy and fulfilled you make a better partner, parent, worker, employee or boss?

Success should feel good and be in alignment with who you are. We each have a purpose and a specific reason for being here. When we are off track it doesn't feel right in our gut. Growing up, we're often told what to do, what to want, what goals to attain. Take a look at why we would be taught that. Who benefits? Our parents, our employers, our government . . . and that's fine—as long as it's your definition of success, too.

Goals can and will change throughout your lifetime and it may be difficult to give up something you were taught would bring you happiness when it is actually slowly killing you. You may see your investment of time and sweat equity as lost or you may take the lessons and apply them to something else.

We've all seen people absolutely miserable trying to get to some externally created societal goal; they'll stay in a job they hate that's causing them physical pain or emotional stress so they can obtain retirement benefits. We've also seen people whose definition of success is peace of mind and living on their own terms off the grid or out of the bounds of society. Somewhere in between there's a sweet spot that will not only feel good when you get there, but can feel good most of the way there!

- Get clear on your definition of success (your personal, individual definition). Write it down and keep it someplace you can see it daily, taped to a mirror or on your computer monitor.

- When you see someone else succeed, what does it bring up for you? Jealousy? Criticism? Do you measure yourself against them? As you get more clear and sure-footed on your journey, you'll only have good wishes for them.

- If you set and track goals, assess them against your personal definition of success.

- Keep score of the game you are playing—not anyone else's game.

- Recognize that priorities and goals will shift, as will your definition of success.

- Don't allow anything to hinder your reinvention—if goal-setting and tracking isn't your thing, let it go. Track progress based on changes in how you feel and what you see around you.

Ask Yourself:

- What are your personal values?

- What motivates you?

- How do you keep score?

- What do you want to include in your scoreboard?

- What milestones do you see on your path to reinvention? And when will you really start to know you're getting there?

CHAPTER 9:
WHAT'S YOUR STORY?

Our stories are very powerful components of who we are. They define us and yet can often bog us down. We develop our stories over our entire lifetimes; sometimes we even pick up on other people's stories and call them our own. This chapter is about listening to the stories you're telling yourself and others about your life and deciding whether they are working for you or if they need to change. It's about knowing whether it's truly YOUR story and one that serves you or an old story from a long time ago that you've been dragging around and is holding you back. This is about letting go of worn-out stories and focusing on stories of how you want your life to be. It's about redefining yourself with a new story that is about the person you are truly meant to be.

—Andria

Andria's Story

The past does not equal the future unless you live there. —Tony Robbins

KISS YOUR PAST GOODBYE

What's your story? Do you have a consistent story or one that varies based on what day it is? The fact is we all have many stories about our lives—stories about our relationships, our careers, our finances, our children, our bodies, our health, our childhood and so many other things. The stories we tell others and ourselves tend to define who we are and how we live our lives.

What are the themes of the stories you tell? Are they tales of triumph? Defeat? Are they factual? Embellished?

Typically we create our stories based on the events we experience throughout our lives. They are stories of our past that we carry with us, which, in turn, makes them stories of our present that will define and create our future. And as you tell stories of the past, you drag them with you into your future. This keeps you in a continuous loop of re-creating your past. Are your stories of the past empowering you? In order to let go of your status quo, you must let go of the stories from your past that are holding you there. Create new stories that empower you, stories about the future version of you—live for your future and leave your past behind.

When I was in the midst of my second divorce and going through my self-pity phase, you already know how I spent quite a few Saturday afternoons lying in bed with the shades drawn. I remember one afternoon I was drifting in and out of sleep and half listening to a talk show rerun on TV. A woman was talking about her difficult life as a single mom raising three kids and what a constant struggle it was to get by. The discussion was about whether we share life facts or life *truth* and how this shapes the stories we tell about ourselves.

The special guest (who I believe was an author) told the single mom she was telling a story that didn't serve her well. She said the facts were she was a single mom of three but the truth is what she makes of those facts. Did she want her truth to be that life was a constant struggle? If so, the story she was telling was in support of that truth. If she wanted her truth to be that she was a strong, capable and amazing woman because she was raising three kids on her own, then her story needed to reflect that new truth.

I remember vaguely thinking (as I tried to fall back to sleep) that the facts and truth of my life are one in the same—*I am a twice-divorced woman who is a complete failure at relationships. End of story.* At that time, that was my truth because of how I interpreted the facts of my life. I accepted that story as my truth back then, but thankfully it was a truth I eventually decided to change.

Yes, the facts remain that I was married and divorced twice, but today the truth is that those relationships and their demise don't define me. They weren't right for me and were difficult but necessary learning experiences required for me to become the woman I am today. Today that is my truth and therefore the story I tell about those life experiences. It took me a while to change my story about my relationship past, but it was a necessary step to take so I could re-create my future relationship. Hanging on to that story would have kept me in my past, and would have kept me from creating a new future. That's why it's so important to examine the stories we tell and how they are impacting our lives.

Our stories are very powerful. Oftentimes they define our lives and who we are. We identify with our stories, so changing one can be a big deal because it changes how we identify ourselves. Stories can also be excuses. If I stuck by my story that I was a failure at relationships, it would have been a good excuse to never take a risk on another relationship again. And it would have been an even better excuse if another relationship failed. Yet I didn't want that to be my truth, so I took the facts of what happened in my life and turned them into a new truth. My new story came from the place of wanting a different type of relationship in the future. It came from a place of wanting to re-create my relationship experience.

What are some of your stories? Do they revolve around your childhood? Your career? Your body? Your finances? Are they stories that support the person you want to be—or the person you were ten years ago?

As already noted, stories can keep us stuck. They are very closely aligned with our internal self-chatter. Our stories can also vary depending on the people with whom we share them. I know that when I communicate with certain people in my life, I can fall back into old habits of how I tell my story. For example, there are some people in my life that I've told a very balanced story to, which means I shared the good *and* the bad. I believe I shared my story this way because it was habitual and worked well for these relationships. It was expected, yet for me it was a very old story.

The reason I continued to tell my old story to certain people is because something inside me believed that in order to keep the relationships thriving, I needed to tell my old story. I was concerned that if I was too positive about my life and didn't balance that with enough negativity, these people might feel bad. So there I was, taking responsibility for how others might feel because of my life choices and experiences. Despite the fact that I knew that I wasn't responsible for how anyone else feels, I still told my old story for *them*.

180

Minimizing my new story for the sake of how someone else might feel kept me bogged down in my old story and, in a sense, kept me from truly letting go of what I needed to let go of to move forward in my journey.

Do you experience this in your life? When are you minimizing your story to appease others? And are you appeasing others or appeasing yourself?

I realized that I had some of my own insecurities about sharing my new story with certain people because of my familiar fear of "What will they think?" *What will they think if they hear that my business is thriving? Will they think I'm bragging? What will they think when they find out I'm taking my fifth vacation this year? Will they think that's extravagant? What will they think when they hear we're moving to a bigger house on eleven acres of land?*

Obviously I had many old stories consisting of others thinking negatively of me because of my successes. I was assuaging my own fears of their thinking badly of me by minimizing my new story. Again I flashed back to what my mentor told me many years ago: "What they think of me is none of my business."

Whose stories are you telling? Looking back at how my stories have evolved, I find I adopted others' stories and made them my own. For example, I told the story of what it meant to be professionally successful so many times that I still find myself reciting it in my head. That story was: "I am a highly successful leader because I work for a big company in corporate America." My story was also that I was successful because I did whatever my company wanted whenever they wanted me to do it.

By watching my dad and other mentors who climbed the corporate ladder before me, I learned that this was a sure way to get ahead and be successful: Never say no. And if you had to say no, you could probably do it once without it derailing your career, but you never said no twice. They ask you to move? You say yes. They ask you at the last minute to get on a plane to fly across the country tomorrow? Yes. It didn't matter what hoops you needed to jump through or what plans needed to change. Yes was the right answer. This was a story I made my own because I had seen it work for others and believed it to be true.

Eventually I realized this was not my story but my dad's story. I adopted it as mine, not because he asked me to (I'm sure he had no idea!) but because I observed it, internalized it, and made it a habit. When I decided to leave the corporate world I finally recognized I'd been telling Dad's story as my own. In order to successfully launch my own company, I had to change this story. This, like when you start changing the internal voice track playing in your head, can feel awkward at first. I wanted my new story to be that I was a highly successful business owner so I told it despite how awkward it felt.

Eventually this new way began to resonate but there were still many parts of my old story that crept back into my life. Letting go of the habit of constantly saying yes in my work world continues to be challenging. As I mentioned earlier, I continued to declare that my success was the result of always saying yes to whatever my employer or client asked of me. Changing this to something that resonated more with the businesswoman I wanted to be was essential for me to cease dragging my past into my future. Now my story is that, at C3, we serve our clients to the best of our ability in a way that is mutually beneficial.

In the beginning this felt a lot like getting a new haircut. You feel different, perhaps lighter, and when you look in the mirror you may be surprised to see how different you look… yet, you like it.

It's the same thing with new stories. They feel different and sometimes they surprise you when you start telling them, but you like them so you stick with them. The more comfortable you get with your new stories, the ones that allow you to let go of your status quo and redefine yourself as the person you want to be, the more powerful they become.

Old stories, like negative self-talk, can hold us back. The longer we've been telling a story, the more we identify with it and the harder it is to let go—like how, when my parents were in the midst of their divorce, I made a promise to myself that I would never, ever be dependent on anyone or have them take care of me. That was an agreement I made with myself at age thirteen and was the beginning of a very powerful story. The story started "I am an independent woman."

That, in and of itself, would have been a great story. Mine went beyond that. It turned into "I am an independent woman who has to take care of and do everything myself or it won't get done." That may be a common story for many women; we feel like we must take care of everything or it won't get done, or it won't get done the way we would do it (which, of course, is the right way).

The older I get, the more I realize that this is an exhausting way to live. However, this was a very strong promise I made to myself (at a vulnerable age) that lived on for over two decades. Letting go of it meant letting go of a piece of what makes me who I am. At the same time, I wanted and knew it needed to change. Instead of tossing it all out and pretending it never existed, I acknowledged that it was a promise and an agreement that was now fulfilled. I kept that promise to myself and was ready to make a new one.

The new story started the same as the old one: "I am an independent woman." The new part of the story says, "who doesn't have to or want to do everything on her own and readily accepts help when it's needed." It felt like a new haircut for a while, and at times it still does. As I am writing this and getting ready to move my home and my family, I find myself automatically thinking I have to do everything to get our current house ready to be sold, do everything to get us ready to move, to move the animals, move our household goods, and, oh yes, run my business at the same time. I must regularly remind myself that this is an OLD story.

As I remind myself, I actually step back to allow the necessary support. I step away and let Matt move the heavy boxes and do half of the packing. I take the physical steps required to support my new story.

This is another good way to help change your stories: take action in the direction of your new story. Moving towards what it is you want to create in your life helps the self-talk and new stories become more real. Sometimes just repeating it to yourself or saying it out loud is not enough. Taking small actions that align with the new story creates a feeling of it being real.

Watching Matt haul boxes to the car reminds me that one reason our relationship is a success is because I learned to tell a new story about relationships. I had to do this since the one I had been telling myself about my lousy track record was so palpable for so many years. Just saying that I could be a success at a long-term relationship was not enough. I had to physically move in that direction to make my new story real. I did this one small step at a time. I didn't want the facts of my two divorces to define my relationship future, so I moved in a different direction and told a new story.

What stories are you telling about yourself? Are they supportive of where you are headed? Are your actions supportive of the life you want to create?

Our old stories can be self-sabotaging but we don't recognize it because they are comfortable. It's like the old pair of slippers or sweatpants that we adore because they create so much comfort and feel so familiar. Old stories are the same way, they are comfortable and familiar. They keep us secure in the status quo. It's similar with people who stay in dysfunctional relationships. They know how to function in that environment and their stories support this. Despite how difficult it may seem to an outsider, it actually works for them. I know because I was in dysfunctional relationships in the past and remained because they were familiar and comfortable.

To re-create your life, your stories must change to support the new life you are creating. It takes a lot of courage to change your story, shed your comfortable layer and step into something new. Taking action aligned with the new story increases your comfort with what you're stepping into and the story that supports it. It helps you separate yourself from the old stories that aren't serving you well. So much of the status quo is wrapped around stories we tell and may have been telling for years. Let go of those stories that are not serving you well. Let go of the stories that are not your own. You will soon find yourself letting go of the status quo.

It's not just about a new story, it's about a new identity. —Tony Robbins

WHAT'S YOUR STORY?

- What stories are you telling? Are they holding you back or empowering you?

- Think about some stories from your family of origin—certain memories that flash in your mind about your parents, your siblings, and your friends. Sometimes there's a takeaway that you received that's not accurate or is not assisting you in life. For example, my old stories were that a successful personal life meant marriage and children by the time I was thirty years old. Are your stories your own or those you've picked up from others throughout your life? Be sure you are not carrying someone else's belief and burden.

- Create empowering stories that speak about the version of you that is currently evolving: the *you* that you're creating. Imagine it, feel it, dream it. Make it as palpable as possible and use it to replace your old negative thoughts when they come up.

- Step away from the stories that no longer serve you and begin telling the stories of your future self, from the energy of your future self.

- Take action to support your new stories; movement in the direction of your new stories makes them more powerful and real. Even one small step can be significant.

CHAPTER 10:
GETTING IT ALL AT ONCE

You probably have a vision of what you'll be like once you have finished your journey of reinvention. This will happen or that will happen. Everything will fall into place and be perfect. No more surprises. This chapter will reinforce that sometimes the best part of the journey is the unknown. It can be so much better than you ever dreamed possible.

—Julie

Julie's Story

I've never had a dream go this far, so I can't really say it's a dream come true.

—*Bubba Watson, 2012 Masters Champion*

TWICE BLESSED

I'm not a golfer, however when I heard Bubba Watson's quote about winning the 2012 Masters Golf Tournament, I could completely relate. Have you ever had something so much bigger than you expected occur? Something beyond your wildest dreams? My journey of reinvention took me down a path I never imagined and I am so much better for it.

Now you know my story of going from child-free by choice to wanting a child, to losing a child, and then finally getting pregnant with the help of fertility specialists. From my experience I thought the most challenging part of becoming a mother was going to be getting pregnant. I was in for a surprise!

Greg and I seemed to talk exclusively baby from the moment we found out we were pregnant. We discussed our hopes, dreams and goals for our child and our parenting approach. Oh, that was fun: two blissfully ignorant parents telling each other what they were going to do in hypothetical parenting situations. I only wish I had a recording of those discussions!

In the dark, quiet moments when I was alone with my thoughts, I acknowledge I was scared to death we would lose this pregnancy. Even though I knew there was little I could do to control it, I wanted to do whatever I could to ensure we had a healthy baby delivered full-term. We were fortunate to have the incredible support of our fertility

190

specialist but I still wasn't confident by any stretch of the imagination. He recommended, due to the previous miscarriage and my age, that we have an ultrasound at the nine-week mark to ensure the viability of the fetus. Typically they wait to do an ultrasound until later in the pregnancy, but in my case we had the bonus of seeing the baby up close and personal early. I didn't have any pregnancy symptoms and was slightly concerned about the health of the baby, so it was refreshing to know we'd see things sooner than twenty weeks.

Happily Greg and I returned to the fertility specialist's office on a cool, bright fall morning. We were escorted into the exam room and waited in the office with intense excitement for the doctor and nurse to arrive. The doctor spent a few minutes conducting the examination. The room was excruciatingly quiet, which is difficult for an extrovert to handle. My mind began to race with thoughts of all the possibilities: *Was the baby okay? Was it growing? Was there a heartbeat? Please, God, let the baby be okay. We can handle anything as long as the baby is okay.* I was completely unprepared for the news we were about to hear.

After several minutes of awkward silence, the doctor began to review the ultrasound with us. "This is the amniotic sack. Here is the heartbeat. Nice and strong, what you'd expect. Measuring right on track for this stage in the pregnancy."

I remember letting out an audible sigh. Thank goodness everything was fine. Glad we are on track. Everything is progressing as expected. My mind immediately moved on to the next activity for the day. I wondered how traffic would be given the time of day and how quickly I thought I could make it back to the office. I had two big meetings and this appointment had already taken longer than I expected. *If I time this right, I can avoid all the traffic and be back in the office in twenty minutes. Let's wrap this up, Doc.*

I was about to start getting up from the exam table when the doctor moved the wand. "And this is the second heart beat. Here is the second amniotic sack. Again, measuring right on track. Exactly what we would expect at this stage. Congratulations, you are having twins!"

Wait. Rewind. What was that? Did he say TWINS? It simply didn't even register with me. I was still processing the success of our first round of IUI since I was convinced it would fail given our low odds. I simply didn't even consider that we might have more than one baby. I was so focused on only being 30 percent of the ideal candidate for IUI that I simply forgot the possibility of multiples. Greg and I certainly discussed the impact fertility had to increase our odds for multiples, but since our weak test results prior to the transfer I assumed if we got pregnant it would surely be only one baby. The room literally went black for a moment.

"Wait a minute, Doctor. You were just looking at the same sack, right? There aren't two babies in there." I found myself suddenly advising the experienced physician about how to read a sonogram. Yet again my type A personality was taking over!

"Julie, I assure you I've been doing this a long time. There are two babies. Two separate sacks. Fraternal twins. Congratulations!"

I was stunned. I looked over to see that Greg was smiling from ear to ear. He was so excited! There aren't many times in your life when you get to see pure, unadulterated surprise and I was able to witness Greg in that very state. It is a moment unlike any other I've ever experienced. Fortunately Greg found his voice quickly and asked, "You must see this all the time. Are twins common?"

The doctor responded, "Not really, especially with the reduced odds you had going into the IUI transfer. You two are just really lucky!" The doctor told us to head over to the office across the hall to see the printed pictures when we were ready.

As soon the doctor and nurse left us, I immediately burst into tears. The magnitude of the news began to sink in and I was totally overwhelmed. How in the world were we going to handle two babies at the same time? We discussed easing into parenthood. We were going to take one step at a time, get pregnant, have a baby, and then decide if we wanted more than one child. Surely two adults could handle one baby, but a man-to-man defense required a whole new strategy. How could we pay for college for two kids at the same time? Forget college, can you imagine the cost of full-time day care for two infants? How in the world would this work? Greg had never even changed a diaper!

It was all too much for me to process. In that moment I realized the possibility of having more than one baby *should* have crossed my mind prior to the appointment. I simply didn't think we would have more than one baby given how cautious our physician had been about our odds when we did the transfer. Fortunately, God reminded me, yet again, of my best life decision ever. Greg was all in! He assured me this would all be okay and it would work out. Lots of people do this and we could handle this gift. God blessed us with twins and Greg was up for the challenge.

Clearly my type A planner personality was in overdrive and I was melting down with the magnitude of the news. Greg said, "I'll give you one week to freak out. You can stress, process the information, and ask all the hypothetical questions you want. Then, after a week, we are all in. This is great! You only have to be pregnant once and we will get two babies! How lucky are we?" And with that, in his mind we were parents of twins. He never, not for one second, looked

back. He embraced fatherhood, times two, from the minute we found out. Greg would, in that very moment, become the rock I never knew I needed.

After I regained my composure, we moved into the small office where we met with the nurse regarding prenatal care. She gave us our first baby pictures of Baby A and Baby B. She provided us with information on additional testing options available. More decisions. It was the beginning of a journey I never imagined I would find myself on as a "mother of multiples." As we looked at the first pictures of our babies we transformed as parents. We were never again parents of one baby. Our minds immediately shifted from one to two.

That week I gave myself the much needed time to transition my preconceived notions about being a parent of one child to the reality of having twins, including endless conversations with Greg about how it would work. After my adjustment week, the focus shifted from panic and anxiety to successfully getting the twins through a full-term twin pregnancy. We took one week at a time. Each week we would focus on a different aspect of preparing for their arrival. My focus became delivering two healthy babies at thirty-eight weeks, full-term for twins. Given my age and the higher risk of carrying multiples, it became imperative to keep my stress level as low as possible.

For the next few weeks I tackled this life change as I had every other challenge in my life: I armed myself with knowledge and developed a plan. I leveraged resources recommended to me by others (parents of multiples support groups, websites, books) and relished the challenge God placed in our hands. Not in a million years when I imagined my life would I have ever thought I would be a mother to twins. I can honestly say it is the most significant accomplishment I (well, we) have ever achieved.

As with any challenge, it is important to understand and embrace what you can control and give up what is beyond your control. I could eat well, get plenty of rest, reduce my stress levels, and still have preterm babies. There was no guarantee my behavior would result in two healthy, full-term babies. I can only say the power of positive thinking, prayer and support from others enabled me to be confident I was doing the best I could to provide the best possible environment for nurturing our twins.

In a matter of four weeks in 2010, Greg and I had enough excitement for a lifetime. One week we found out we were finally pregnant after nearly two years of trying. The next week I secured the position I'd worked for fifteen years to attain. The third week we found out we were having twins! And finally in the fourth week, my dream job slipped out of my hands and I started my own business. We were on the roller-coaster ride of a lifetime!

Looking back, there was nothing I could have done to prepare for those four weeks. I've often reflected on what got me through the highs and lows of that month. First and foremost, my faith in God literally pulled me through the lows and allowed me to rejoice in the highs. I knew there was nothing God could put in front of me He didn't think I could handle. Whether or not I thought I was capable of handling the challenges was another story. I knew God had the confidence in me to be a mother to twins. I knew Greg would be an amazing father and having twins was clearly in God's plan for us. In some strange way I felt God wanted us to be certain we were ready to be parents and part of the miscarriage process was for us to align our goals. And, fortunately, having twins only solidified our need to be on the same page.

I was reminded again of God's unconditional love when my perfect job evaporated two days before I was supposed to start. Remember how I described falling to my knees when I got that call from my new employer? Well, at that very moment I felt God literally embrace me.

195

There was a calm that came over me. I began to catch my breath and immediately He reminded me of the two souls I was incubating. My heart rate slowed and my breathing returned to normal. I knew my #1 priority at this point in my life was to take these two babies as close to thirty-eight weeks as possible. God told me He would take care of the rest. And He did. It is as simple as that.

From that moment on I turned to my faith to guide me. Whenever I would get anxious or stressed, or was faced with a challenge, I would remind myself that God would provide. I can testify He has exceeded my wildest dreams. From the depths of a miscarriage to the heights of delivering two healthy babies at thirty-seven weeks, six days, God has blessed me.

The plan I had in mind for my life was simply not going to be my reality. Despite my best efforts, my career was taking a turn I hadn't expected. Simultaneously, my visions of being a mother were also being magnified. We were going to have twins and I just started my own business. I couldn't have imagined my current life in those moments, yet looking back now I can see the plan God created exclusively for us.

I didn't see any other option but to simply keep moving forward. I had to dig deep and find the inner confidence to turn the lemons into lemonade. Nobody was going to show me the road map to success, either from a parenting perspective or from a career standpoint. I simply had to push myself forward; there was no other alternative.

I began my career as an entrepreneur strictly as a result of unforeseen circumstances. At this point I know it was the absolute right decision for us, however, like most things, it took getting through the difficult patch to have the appropriate perspective. I learned it's wise to allow some time to pass before you evaluate whether or not something is successful. Not all things are easily measured. The really right things may take time to fully evaluate.

I now have the perspective to appreciate that owning my own business affords us the flexibility we need to manage our family. My journey has helped me understand—at the most central level—that there is no such thing as perfection. I've learned to revise my vision of perfection to reflect what is actually attainable.

I thought I'd work at a company as a VP of HR. I'm now the managing director of a woman-owned business. I thought Greg and I would have a child. We have two amazing children. I can't imagine our lives without the twins. Would I ever have imagined being a mother of twins? No, I couldn't dream that big. I came into the role of mother with significant doubts about my abilities. To be honest, those doubts rise up occasionally and I'm sure they will always be there just below the surface. I've learned to accept my vulnerabilities. My journey of reinvention was to have twins and I'm exponentially better off for it. Yes, it is difficult. The first few months are a blur, for good reason, but each and every day I learn something new about my children, my partner or myself. Because I'm equipped to listen to the messages along the way, the journey is so much more enjoyable. I embrace the unknown in ways I never would have prior to starting my journey of letting go of the status quo.

You can achieve your goals; they just may not look exactly as you envisioned them. Remove the limits to your dreams! You may just find out you are capable of bigger things, deeper highs and possibly darker lows. Isn't that what life is all about? Feeling, doing and embracing every aspect it has to offer?

GETTING IT ALL AT ONCE

Sometimes God, the Universe, our Greater Self, has something in mind for us that is bigger than we ever could imagine. This is urging us on to stretch in many ways, to reach the potential we truly have. It is up to us to see this as a burden, a challenge, or a blessing. How many people really get the opportunity to live up to their highest potential?

Right now, take that opportunity, at least in your private world, to imagine what this life would be like.

- If you could dream the biggest dream for your life, what would it look like? Close your eyes and envision it, feel it, really spend time with it. As you connect and reconnect with that feeling, you are easily leading yourself into that state that can become a reality.

- What terrifies you about taking the first step towards your dream? It's good to confront what holds you back, then it doesn't dwell there to hit you when you least expect it. Writing a list of your fears allows you to really examine them and see that most of them are truly outlandish and the probability of them happening is slim. By looking at your fears head on, you are giving yourself the gift of being able to "run them" rather than having them "run you."

- Are you prepared for the landscape to look significantly different? There is a greater consciousness that guides us and co-creates with us. It doesn't always look like what we imagined— sometimes it's better. At first it may not appear that way to you. Sometimes we're asked to let go of a lesser version of ourselves that would be too restricting for our souls and open up to something bigger and better; it just doesn't look as familiar and comfortable as we imagined, so it may take a while to get used to how it looks and how big a change and blessing it actually is. But know it would not have appeared if you were not ready for it, so step up and claim it!

CHAPTER 11:
THERE IS NO FINISH LINE

When you started this book, you were at the starting line, the beginning of the journey where you were recognizing that things were not okay as they were. Now you are at the end of the book and have hopefully made strides in your transformation and letting go of the status quo; however, there is no finish line or final destination. The journey continues because that is what life is, a journey for you to enjoy, cherish, thrive in and create as best fits you. The joy is in the journey and in the twists and turns that arise along the way. The joy is in the fact that there is no finish line, because that means you cannot get it wrong; as long as you keep moving forward and taking steps to do what's best for you, your success is inevitable.

—Julie & Andria

Andria's Story

Life is not about finding yourself, it's about creating yourself. —George Bernard Shaw

LOVE WHERE YOU ARE AND KEEP CREATING IT WITH LOVE

Re-creating yourself and reinventing yourself is a life-long process. Maybe that's not what you wanted to hear. Perhaps you were hoping it was a once-and-you're-done deal but that's not true or real. Life is constant change; things change, people change, and YOU change. That's why the quote at the start of the chapter says, "Life is about creating yourself." Life is designed to keep moving and keep you moving along with it. If you think about it, nothing stays the same, does it? Our bodies change constantly, seasons change, people change; change is the natural order of things. We're designed to continue to grow and evolve, and often it's when we resist the change or resist the feelings that are pulling us towards a change that we create consternation in our lives.

The years I spent resisting, ignoring and pushing aside the internal messages I received about needing to change my personal life situation and needing to let go of my corporate job to create my business were years of inner turmoil for me. I resisted the need (and my calling) to make big changes in my life so I could evolve into the person I was meant to be.

As I am writing this, I am in year three of being a business owner and the changes that have taken place in my business from year one to year two to today are considerable. It's a continuous evolution. In my first year of business, I was marketing C3 as an executive coaching and human resources consulting firm. We took on any type of work for any type of client and ended up with a lot of HR consulting work. After I reconsidered why I started the business, I realized that was not where I wanted us to be focused.

Year two was about redefining the reason I launched C3. I shifted from marketing us as an HR consulting firm and, with the help of marketing and communications experts, rebranded us as a leadership and career development coaching and consulting firm. Year three continues the evolution as we hone in more specifically on the types of clients who most benefit from our services.

I know C3 will continue to evolve as long as we're in business. Not only do the needs of our clients change, but our own expertise grows and changes as well. It is when we resist these changes that things can get stagnant. Trying to hold on to "what is" keeps us knee deep in "what is." Being open to the constant flow of change creates more and more opportunity for us as a company. The same holds true for you. The more you are open to changes, the more opportunities arise for you.

Throughout my journey I've adopted a powerful action that helps me accept the inevitable change and evolution of my life. It is the action of making decisions based upon the life I want; that is, acting as if what needs to change is already a done deal and the life I want to create already exists. When you do this, you truly take the leap; it's about stepping into the person you want to be and the life you want to have and making decisions today, from that new place. Doing this begins to create your future, today.

All your power is in the present moment—it's all you have, so when you make a decision from the present moment that reflects your new perspective, you truly let go of the status quo. Making decisions from where you are or where you once were keeps you stuck there.

Step out of where you are and into where you want to be and you will see magic begin to happen. You will begin to realize that you are already everything you want to be, which helps you get more comfortable with this idea that there is no finish line, only a continuing evolution of your journey

Making decisions based on the life you really want is powerful and helps you re-create your life and let go of the status quo. For the past year, Matt and I have been looking to move to a much bigger home, with a lot more land so we can spread out a bit and rescue more animals. A lot of homes we've fallen in love with have slipped away from us for one reason or another. So how do you act "as if" what you want is already present when in reality it seems to keep slipping away from you? That is the question I've been asking myself the past several months.

There is an element of faith that comes into play here. You have to believe and have faith that what you really want can be yours—that the change will be for the best and that the life you want does exist. For me, faith is a huge part of how I live my life and make decisions. I put a lot of faith in what may seem unknown but deep down I know is right for me

In between the varying levels of frustration I experienced when watching not one or two, but three seemingly perfect homes slip away from us, I reminded myself that they must have slipped away because there is something much better waiting for us. I had to believe that these homes weren't right and have faith that the best one for us was still out there. I decided to be diligent and practice making decisions from the future place where I was headed. I knew that I wanted to be living in a home on many acres of land in the middle of the country, in a less congested area. And I knew I wanted relocate my business. I had to begin to make decisions from this place instead of from where I was presently sitting.

As I worked in my current home office, I opened the windows and imagined that that the traffic I heard in the distance was really wind blowing through the trees. I put up pictures of the scenery I imagined would be visible from our new home and I began to "act as if" we were moving. What would I do if we were moving? I'd start to clean out and pack. So that's what I did. I began cleaning closets, donating, and preparing our current home to be sold and packed up to move. I also began making business decisions that reflected a relocation of our headquarters. I got an 800 number and began shifting my business model to one that would work more effectively from the new location.

If you looked at our house and the decisions I made on a daily basis, you would think, "She's getting ready to move." And you know what? You'd be right.

Within two months of taking those actions, I am happy to say Matt and I are getting ready to settle on our dream home and will be moving in less than two months. I acted from a place of faith and knowing that I want to be living in a different part of the country and running my business from there. I acted in faith knowing that the reason things hadn't worked out with several other homes the past year was because there was something better for us. And this place that we are moving into is actually better than the previous three we thought were perfect.

It's truly amazing what can happen when you act from a place of belief and faith and when you know that no matter what you see in front of you, everything is always working out perfectly. I could have chosen to wallow in the fact that our (seemingly) perfect homes kept getting away from us. And I did wallow in that for some time. But that wouldn't have done anything to help us get different results or change our situation. Acting as if we were moving and making decisions that would be made if we were moving created the results we were looking for—we *are* moving.

Depending on your specific situation and where you are sitting right now, this may sound futile and you may not think it's possible to make decisions differently from the way you do today. That's why I suggest baby steps. You cannot get different results if you keep doing the same things. So start making small changes and I bet you will see small changes in your results. Ask yourself what you truly want your evolution to look like. Believe you can have it. Know that you deserve it. It will be yours as you begin to let go of your status quo and make decisions from the place where you want to be. As you do this it's important to remember to enjoy each step of your evolution and not race to the end. There is no hurry because there truly is no finish line; your life will continue to evolve as long as you are living it!

It takes courage to step up into a life change and into the person you desire to be and are meant to be. This idea of life being constant change can be scary, but it can also be exhilarating. When I was much younger and working at one of my first jobs after graduate school, the company was reorganizing, and during a meeting one of the senior leaders made a side comment to me about the change. He said, "I always tell people that if you don't like the way things are changing now, don't worry. It'll all change again in six months."

I liked that concept. What a blessing change is. If you don't like the way things are, no worries—they will be different soon enough. Early on in my career I came to expect change and saw it as opportunity. Whether the change involved a new leadership team, new customers, or a new merger or acquisition, these things always created opportunities.

But what if you like the way things are and don't want them to change? That's perfectly fine too—however, despite how much you love the way things are now, change is inevitable. Your children continue to grow up, you continue to age and get wiser, seasons change and adaptation is required. Adaptation doesn't necessarily mean a life change or an entire reinvention, but the idea is to be comfortable with the natural changes that happen in life so that when you do get pulled to make a big change or want to re-create your life, you will accept it and approach it as a blessing and an opportunity to become a better, more evolved version of you.

Changes in both my business and personal life that happen today are the result of my constantly focusing more and more on what I want. It's like my experiences are a buffet, and from that selection of life experiences I decide which ones I want more of and which I do not. Non-ideal, high-maintenance clients? I only had to experience that once before deciding that I don't want them anywhere near C3. Waking up too many consecutive days feeling a sense of not wanting to get up? I've learned that it can and will last as long as I let it, so I quickly decide to alter what I'm doing and how I'm spending my time to something more enjoyable and inspiring. It doesn't have to be anything big but something that makes a difference.

You'd think that after spending the past number of years re-creating both my personal and professional life I'd be ready to just sit back and enjoy it. Well, I am thoroughly enjoying it and part of that enjoyment comes from my comfort with the change and movement that is happening around me and within me. But I don't want to sit back because the more I change and grow and experience life and all I'm meant to be doing, the more I can share my experiences with others. The more I evolve, the more I can help others let go of their status quo and step into who they are truly meant to be.

As I have taken risks and leapt into the unknown, I have experienced the blessings of many people along the way who have shared their stories and triumphs with me, who have encouraged me and cheered me on. It is through my own life changes and reinventions that I have come to a place where I can truly help others in the same way I have been helped and supported. When I was living my life based on old stories, old habits, and fear of what others would think if I wanted to change my life, I wasn't in a place of truly being able to give back and help others. It wasn't until I learned to fully give to myself and love myself enough to do what was best for me that I was able to fully give to others.

This goes back to putting your own oxygen mask on first before assisting others. I had to fully give to myself and feel complete so I had plenty to give to others. If you're on empty, what is there to give anyone else? Being able to help and support others who are less fortunate or in situations like those I experienced is also a way for me to continue my own journey and evolution. It doesn't matter how far I've come and how much I've changed my life, I always learn something new and add to my journey through the stories of others and my ability to help others.

What are you experiencing in your life? Are you in a place where you have enough to give to others?

If not, fully give to yourself and take care of yourself first, and then reach out to others to serve and support them and share your gifts. As you do, you will also be receiving and feeding your own continued journey. You will see yourself in others and continue to learn more about yourself through what you see in those you are supporting. It is all part of our continued collective life journey.

I've experienced change in my life as a domino effect. Once something changes significantly, it has impact on other areas of my life. The changes that happened in my personal life after my second divorce directly led to the changes that happened in my professional life. After I met Matt and was in an honest, strong and growing relationship with him, I began to realize that there was a lot more I wanted to do and experience outside of working all the time.

208

Launching C3 was a way for me to get more control over how I spent my time so I could have a more balanced life.

Re-creating and improving your life in one area will naturally make other areas that are not aligned with your newly defined self stand out more. Address those areas and get them in alignment with your new definition of you. It's not as if everything around you requires you to change, but as your life continues to move forward you must evolve to move with it. It truly is a continuous journey and one that's about constant creation of *you*.

We were designed to continue to grow and evolve. It's why things are always changing. Each part of the journey, each element that we've discussed in this book, is a continual part of the process of creating your life by design. Each element is to help you enjoy your journey and not resist your calling to let go of the status quo and step into the life you are meant to have. I have discovered that these things we have written about throughout the book are elements to help you take good care of yourself as you create the life you are longing to live and are meant to have. We each have a unique role to play on this earth and each have unique gifts to share with others. Share your gifts, step into your passions, live YOUR life on YOUR terms. Find your voice and listen to it like no other. Trust yourself and know that in letting go of the status quo, you will step into the realm of unlimited possibilities.

The real point of being alive is to evolve into the whole person you were intended to be.

—*Oprah Winfrey*

Julie's Story

Happiness is a journey, not a destination; happiness is to be found along the way not at the end of the road, for then the journey is over and it's too late. The time for happiness is today not tomorrow. —Paul H. Dunn

REINVENTION NEVER ENDS

Are you reluctant to start your journey of reinvention? Perhaps circumstances outside of your control have forced you to reinvent yourself. Can't wait until you reach the finish line? Along my journey I found myself feeling all of these emotions plus a thousand more. One of the most important lessons my reinvention journey taught me is that there is, unlike most trips, no final destination.

Letting go of the status quo takes time and there is no way around investing the time into the journey. Reinvention isn't something you can simply schedule in your calendar and check off your to-do list. You can, however, take active measures to evolve and move towards your goals. By using the guideposts throughout this book you can increase the speed and impact of your journey.

An interesting thing happened along my way to reinventing myself.

I found the closer I got towards my goals, the more my goals evolved and changed. As I continued to learn and grow, the goals I set for myself also changed. The goal I set three years before simply didn't seem as significant once I attained it. I found myself moving away from career goals and moving towards goals of personal fulfillment.

One of the benefits of my journey of reinvention is learning it is perfectly acceptable to continue to reinvent myself. Again and again. Over and over again. I evolved from a career-minded young professional climbing the corporate ladder to business owner. When I began my journey I was happily single and along the way made the best decision of my life to marry Greg. We then grew from child-free by choice to experiencing the silent battle of infertility and eventually becoming parents of twins. If I could only show the uncertain young woman in her teens and early twenties what an accomplished, compassionate woman she would grow into, I can assure you she wouldn't recognize herself.

The joy of the journey is truly discovering your authentic self and creating your authentic life. Your life should exploit your best attributes while giving you the chance to focus on your priorities, recognizing they may change along your journey. It may take supporting another person on their journey to help you understand yourself more fully. Embrace the opportunities presented to you at face value. You may get burned, but more often than not you will grow from the experiences and become a richer person.

Along my journey I reignited a passion I'd lost over the years. Philanthropy has been one of my core values for as long as I can remember. I am driven to give to others. While I'm far from having a significant amount of money to give away, I do my best to give back to my community. I always dreamed of having the ability to make an impact in the local community. As I continued to focus on my career, I seemed to lose sight of my passion for charitable causes. I was caught up in climbing the corporate ladder and advancing my own professional cause. I found very little access to philanthropic boards and causes given my limited professional contacts.

When I had the opportunity to start my business I knew a core value would be corporate social responsibility. The opportunity was right! I'm the co-chair for the Future Fund, a giving circle of young professionals at the Community Foundation for Northern Virginia. Members of the Future Fund connect with each other personally and professionally, learn about the critical needs of our region, and donate to the philanthropic causes they care about most—a unique and exciting opportunity to pool contributions to benefit the local community.

The more I continue to reinvent myself, the more I find my authentic self. I surround myself with others who are living their authentic lives. The circle continues to expand. We all want to live the most authentic, happy and harmonious lives possible.

The good news is that in this tribe there is always room for one more. We want to welcome you into the fold of the newly reinvented! It is perfectly acceptable not to know who you will be in five years, or five days, for that matter. What isn't acceptable is to give up trying to create your authentic self.

Embrace the anxiety you feel about starting your journey of reinvention. Channel it and allow it to drive you to make a change in your life. Without positive stress propelling you in a new and different direction, nothing will change. None of us have a crystal ball to see what the future holds. We are all on the journey together. You aren't alone in your desire to find a more fulfilled life. The difference between those who achieve the life they want and those who don't is simply action.

Andria and I took action and our lives are all the better because of it. We embraced the fear, took risks, succeeded when faced with doubts and ultimately let go of the status quo.

My journey isn't over yet. As I embark on the second year of my business and the second year of motherhood, both landscapes change drastically. Just when I think I've mastered a client, something changes. When will my next client materialize? I still have my moments of doubt about how I'm running the business. I still question whether I'm doing it correctly. When all is said and done, I finish each day with the confidence that I left it all on the field. I did my best to provide value to my clients.

Concurrently, I'm tested as a mother on a daily basis. The first year seemed to go by in a blink. As any mother of a newborn knows, the days were long but the weeks were short. It seemed like as soon as I figured out the routine, something would change. Once we got the twins to sleep regularly, my son began to teethe. After teething it was time to learn to talk and walk. As I reflect on the first year of motherhood, I am amazed we all survived the chaos. The sleepless nights are a distant memory. Days are now filled with new vocabulary words and seeing the world through four fresh eyes. The perspective of the world through the eyes of my children is a journey I realize I'm privileged to lead.

I never miss an opportunity to remind my children I am new to the mommy role. Fortunately they are eager to help me learn the ropes. My confidence as a mother has increased, which allows me to embrace the unknown that is to come. The good news is things will continue to change and I'll continue to learn from the experiences. And, with any luck, life will continue to surprise me with my journey.

Trust your instincts. You've accomplished much in your life already. You have an amazing journey ahead of you. Hopefully we've provided you with tools you can use as you reinvent yourself to find the fulfillment life has to offer. We can't wait to hear your stories!

THERE IS NO FINISH LINE

- The journey of reinvention simply takes time.

- There is no final destination—the journey is the destination.

- Give of yourself and you will learn more about yourself.

- Goals can change as you grow in your journey.

- Be confident!

- Change is the natural order of life. Change is the only constant. Learn to flow with change.

- The more you are open to changes in your life, the more opportunities arise for you.

- By reaching a place where you can support others along their journeys, you receive the gift of evolving in consciousness through your ability to help others and give back.

- As life continues to naturally progress and change, you must evolve so you can progress with it.

- If you set date-driven goals along your journey, be sure to be flexible as you assess your progress against any self-created time constraints.

- Remember, life is a journey and there is no final destination, so enjoy each and every moment being your wonderful self!

CHAPTER 12:
WHERE AM I NOW?

Andria's Story:

LEAVING "OKAY" BEHIND

As I write the last chapter of this book, I am sitting on the back deck of our new home in Virginia's horse and wine country overlooking the pond on our property. I am surrounded by what seems like endless green, countless trees, and sounds of birds, cicadas, and a distant lawn mower. Matt and I moved to our dream home on eleven acres of land two months ago and we couldn't be happier. We just celebrated our five-year relationship anniversary, which prompted much reflection on how far we have come as a couple, and as individuals.

I look back to how drastically different my life was five years ago and am very proud at how much I have changed and grown and how much I continue to grow each day. Writing this book and sharing my story was a part of that growth. I realize how cathartic it was for me to share my story because it enabled me to accept all aspects of the

217

journey I've taken to get where I am today. And each time I glance at the Table of Contents, I am reminded that the journey never ends; the elements that Julie and I wrote about in each chapter continue to be part of my life, with the exception of one: the very first element we wrote about in Chapter 1, The Starting Line: It's NOT Okay to Just Be "Okay."

Today my life is much more than okay; it is overflowing with an abundance of love and joy. I am beyond blessed to have the relationship I have with Matt and be living the life of a successful business owner. C3 continues to grow and thrive and I am so fortunate to have clients I adore. Yes, things are a lot more than okay; they are wonderful. I also know that because of the journey I took to arrive here, I will quickly recognize if things are not okay and will not allow that to linger because I know how to change it.

The elements we wrote about to let go of the status quo continue to impact how I live my life today. When things need to change in my business or in my personal life, I shift gears and move into first, second or even fifth gear, whatever is necessary! I know all the results I achieve in all areas of my life are a direct result of my taking ownership and guiding myself along my desired path. No one else can do that but me.

I consistently take time to create space in my life to listen to those ever-important internal messages that are always there. I still run every day and now have the added pleasure of running along peaceful country roads where I am more apt to see horses, cows and donkeys than cars. That creates a tremendous amount of meditative space for me to be with me and clear my head so important messages can get through. I continue to remind myself that failure is not an option because I know I can't ever really fail. Yes, making mistakes is inevitable, but the only failures are those when I deny what is best for me. My tribe and extended support systems are still a powerful force in my life and they always will be. I regularly ask for help, yet maintain my independent nature at the same time because it is at the core of who I am. I know that one does not preclude the other.

I continue to struggle with some of the negative self-talk that creeps back into my head. Despite how much progress I've made, I still have many miles to go and work at it daily. I still keep score and I am a stickler for meeting goals and objectives, but I am much more conscious that the scoreboard has been defined and created only by me. It's easy for me to fall back into what others think or how they define success, but my awareness of how this can negatively impact my growth and success keeps me from getting too far into someone else's game and rules.

The fact that I am writing this last chapter from this beautiful, peaceful land that I call home is a testament to how making decisions today for where you want to be tomorrow works. I previously wrote about how I "acted as if" Matt and I were moving before we ever found our new home. I know that set unseen forces into motion and I never stopped preparing for our move despite a few seemingly heartbreaking scenarios with houses slipping away from us.

Looking back, I see it all so clearly now; we are exactly where we are supposed to be. This house is perfect for us, in a perfect location, and the environment enables us to thrive both personally and professionally. This amazing place is why the others fell through. I believe we are here today because we began making decisions to get us here long before it seemed possible or real and, despite all the heartbreak, we never lost faith that the perfect home was waiting for us.

All our power rests in today and I regularly make decisions not based on where I am today, but based on where I intend to be tomorrow. This fuels my story, which is another big part of how I continue to live my life. I tell stories of what can be, what will be, what I want to be as opposed to what is. This keeps me growing and moving forward. Don't get me wrong, I love where I am in my life and cherish each moment, yet I also know I want to continue to evolve, so I look around, and while cherishing what I love about where I am, I expand on that and create my story for tomorrow. Not only is it fun but also it fuels the future with unlimited possibilities. And, my friends, that's really what this is all about: a future that you create filled with unlimited possibilities. It is the journey of you that never ends.

There is no finish line but only a continued path for you to move forth. There is unlimited potential for you on that path, but to get there you, like us, must be willing to let go of the status quo. You, like us, can reinvent yourself and create an amazing life—one that you fit into like a warm, snug glove, one that feels like you've come home. All you need to do is make the decision and take one small step at a time, and before you know it, it will be six years later and you'll look back, like me, and be amazed at the grace and peace you see around you each day.

Wishing you a wonderful journey!

Julie's Story

STRETCHING INTO MY NEW STORY

Today I am at peace. I didn't know this level of contentment existed. In the midst of the most significant changes in life I managed to find the holy grail: peace. As I finish this book the reoccurring theme of peace is abundant in my life. I am no longer restless. It is refreshing to live an authentic life each and every day! I find myself more confident in my decisions because of the framework Andria and I shared in this book.

My journey has taught me to embrace the present, for it is far too fleeting and this phase will pass quickly. My children dominate my scoreboard. Gone are the crazy days of sleeplessness with twin newborns. Stella and Will are full toddlers now and embrace every aspect of this stage of growth. They have mastered walking and are developing an extremely diverse vocabulary.

My days are filled with milestones achieved: crawling up the stairs, walking, holding one hand as we cross the street, saying their sibling's name, feeding themselves. These accomplishments are things I couldn't have imagined when we brought them home from the hospital. I find myself pleasantly surprised when our babies reach a milestone. I have mixed emotions of happiness to see my children learning and growing, followed by the sadness of their independence. How can I really miss twenty-four feedings a day and lugging two of those heavy car seat carriers everywhere I went? The lesson I take away from being a mom is that time will march on regardless of how long the present moment seems. In a flash the sweet babies who once slept in my arms swaddled like burritos are replaced with jumping beans who seem to fight endlessly over the same toy.

My confidence as a mother to twins has increased significantly in the past several months. Greg took a much-deserved weekend away with his college friends recently. This was not even a remote possibility when the babies were infants. Despite my anxiety about managing twins alone, I found the joy in the experience. It was remarkably fun to spend time with the twins alone. I read a lot of positive affirmations when the kids were napping! The time away gave me space to reflect on the terrific dad Greg has become as well as how much we've grown as a team.

Over the past year there were several times when I found myself unsure about whether I should continue with my business or simply stay home with my children. It is something mothers continue to struggle with, asking themselves, "Am I making the best decision for my family by _____ [working, staying at home, getting a divorce, staying married]?" I honestly hope in my lifetime we can end the "mommy wars" and simply accept that each family does what is best for them at a given point in time. Isn't it great we live in a country where a Fortune 500 company can hire a CEO who happens to be six months pregnant and that detail isn't even mentioned in the Yahoo press release? Kudos to Yahoo for changing the paradigm for all working women, mothers or not. I've concluded that I enjoy owning my business, and in order to honor my authentic self I'll continue my entrepreneurial expedition.

Creating space to hear the important messages life is sending my way continues to be an integral part of my daily life. I continue to carve out at least fifteen minutes a day without distraction to focus on myself. By honoring myself I'm able to honor the important people in my life. When I'm able to keep a strong focus on myself I'm able to manage the challenges that arise. Whether it is balancing business meetings with family schedules or navigating a parenting pitfall, I'm able to demonstrate agility to manage the stress of the situation. The messages have continued to change as my journey has evolved.

Exercise continues to be an integral part of my life, however it has evolved beyond going to the gym. I am now incorporating my children into my routine. I've found it may not be what I envisioned; however, I can get a great workout with the twins! Nothing like a twenty-five-pound baby on your back to make you feel the burn of a set of lunges! That is the beauty of the journey of reinvention. You can have it all, it just may not look like you imagined it would.

Additionally, I've enhanced my ability to know intuitively when I need to shift gears. Human Capital Strategic Consulting is well into its second year. I find myself managing work and my personal life slightly more successfully. The business continues to grow through referrals, which is humbling. I'm proud of the stellar client service we provide, as demonstrated by the deep partnerships we've developed with our clients. I struggle with knowing what the future holds for my business. Failure is still not an option. I am more confident than ever before that HCSC is exactly where I am supposed to be at this point in my life.

I've been approached to take full-time corporate HR positions at various companies. Each and every time I evaluate what makes sense for me, my family and my business, I again uncover my desire to grow my own business. The risk of entrepreneurship is worth the rewards. I can't say I know which new clients I'll have in the future, but I've learned I will be successful. I'm already successful on my terms, and that makes all the difference.

I've taken the power of my people to heart and expanded my business tribe. I've introduced account managers to help me grow HCSC. I trusted my instincts and listened intently when it became evident my time constraints would affect my ability to grow my business. Slowly I began to evaluate candidates I felt could represent my business and support my clients. I've successfully integrated four amazing women into HCSC. Melissa, Tara, Stefanie and Diana are human resources professionals who share my values, vision and commitment to client service. I relish the opportunity to introduce my clients to these outstanding professionals who represent both my business vision and personal values. I'm honored to be leading a talented consulting team in a way that meets the needs of each individual and client involved.

I've learned your tribe will support you personally and professionally. For me, this meant being completely transparent about my expectations and honoring the expectations of others. My company is stronger with the support of my incredible team. I am blessed to benefit from their talents. Your tribe can surprise you with reinforcement beyond your wildest dreams!

I continue to lead the Future Fund and I'm the vice president of involvement for the George Mason University Alumni Association Board of Directors. I've also been asked to serve on the Board of Visitors for Marymount University. Higher education continues to be an area of personal interest and I'm delighted to have an opportunity to give back to these two unique institutions. I'm able to articulate my scoreboard and it includes being an active member of my community as well as a philanthropist. I'm proud my journey has provided me with the opportunity to demonstrate my personal commitment to enhancing the community in which I live and work.

Most important I find myself fulfilled. I no longer wake up in the morning and dread going to work. I have amazing clients whom I enjoy working with and who value the contribution HCSC makes to their businesses. I enjoy spending time with my children. I relish the variety of my schedule and routine. I've learned that my journey requires me to be exposed to diverse interests. Sharing my story in this book has been cathartic and healing, as well as affirming. I now know I am a Christian, sister, wife, mother, business owner, philanthropist and friend. I've learned to embrace the unknown that life has to offer because the results can be far better than I'd ever imagined. I can't wait to see what God has in store for me.

About the Authors

Julie Simmons, MA, SPHR

Julie is the managing director at Human Capitol Strategic Consulting where she works with organizations to accelerate organizational objectives and drive superior performance through the development and advancement of people. She has over seventeen years of human resources experience in professional services, non-profits, and government contracting organizations.

Julie holds an M.A. in Human Resources from Marymount University and a B.S. in Management from George Mason University. She volunteers in leadership positions with George Mason University, Marymount University, Fairfax Chamber of Commerce, and the Future Fund. She currently lives in Fairfax, Virginia, with her husband, Greg, and their twins, Stella and Will.

Andria Corso, BA, MS

Andria is an award-winning executive leadership and career coach, author and entrepreneur with seventeen years of global business experience. As the owner of C3 Coaching and Consulting, she has worked with a variety of Fortune 100 companies and hundreds of leaders to help them reach their highest potential by developing their leadership skills and talent strategies that align with business strategy and drive results.

In 2009 Andria was given *Training Magazine's* Top Young Trainer of the Year award for her outstanding leadership development programs. She currently lives in Virginia's horse and wine country. *Letting Go of the Status Quo* is her second book.

Andria's Acknowledgements

First I must thank God for without Him I would not have a story to tell.

Thank you to my wonderful friend Julie Simmons. From long before that fateful day sitting in a Bethesda café when she said, "We should write a book together" to today, she has been a huge source of encouragement and inspiration. I know I would not have been able to share my story so authentically without her cheering me on, offering support and motivating me with her huge open heart.

To the wonderful team at Love Your Life Publishing: we would not be here without all your patience and guidance. We are eternally grateful for your wisdom and the good care with which you have handled our book, and us!

Thank you to my tribe – Mom, Debra, Smith. You continue to be my biggest cheerleaders and sounding boards. As you know, you have all played big roles along my journey and I'm happy you're still along for the ride! I adore each of you beyond words.

To my dad—you continue to be the voice of reason, of belief, of encouragement. I'm so grateful for our relationship and for all you continue to teach me.

Nicole, you are my favorite person on this earth. Every day you inspire me with your wisdom, big heart, and authenticity.

I know your journey will be filled with love, peace, wonder, and fun because it will be true to who you are. Remember: if you can believe it, you can achieve it.

To my family, friends, and colleagues who offered support and encouragement along the way... you know who you are! I am beyond blessed to have you in my life.

Huge thank you to Matt, for encouraging me to share my story and continuing to show me what it means to live life on purpose. Words can't express how grateful I am for your unconditional love and support. There's no one else I'd rather be with on this amazing journey of life!

And finally to my favorite critters, Swanny, Lily, Paws, and Philly: thank you for warming my lap and my feet as I wrote this book. You are the pure definition of peace, love and joy and I thank you for showing me that every day.

Julie's Acknowledgements

When you learn, teach, when you get, give. —Maya Angelou

This book is a tribute to the many teachers I've had throughout my life. I am honored to be a part of continuing the endless journey of lifelong learning. Special thanks to my tribe for your faith in my journey when I wasn't even sure I could see a clear path.

Andria Corso, I'm eternally grateful for your passionate belief in our shared goal of living an authentic life. Your warm heart, nurturing spirit, fierce work ethic and beautiful soul have forever impacted my life. I'm honored to be on this life journey with you!

To my Gamma Phi Beta sisters, you truly inspire of a higher type of womanhood. Kari, Windy, Leigh, Amy, Angel, Jen and Calli, thank you for teaching me the values of love, labor, learning and loyalty as they continue to guide me throughout my life's journey. Thanks to the amazing Human Capital Strategic Consulting team for embracing the risk of working with an accidental entrepreneur. Tara, Melissa, Stefanie and Diana, you are true warriors and I'm humbled by your dedication. 2T never looked so good!

My endless gratitude to Lashelle Davis, Steve Gladis, Eileen Ellsworth, Joy Metz, Liana Grassi, Lori Reed, Debbie Blacher, Beth Newton, Christina Duncan, Meg Nelbach, Becca Rinker, Caroline Garrett and Tara Cash for blazing the trail. Seeing you navigate your own paths gave me the courage to share my stories. Your leadership, friendship and support are truly priceless!

This book would not be possible without my Ohana. God shows his love through our family and I thank Him every day for this unique privilege. Team Ohana!

Kristi, you've shown me how love can build a bridge over and over again in our lives. My fondest childhood memories are with you as my partner in crime. Thank you for being my first teacher and for showing me unconditional love.

Stella and Will, you've made my life complete. Being your mother is truly the most fulfilling, challenging, terrifying and unexpected job I'll ever have. God is good. I wouldn't have missed it for anything. My wish for each of you is to live an authentic life on your terms. Remember what Winnie the Pooh says: "You are braver than you believe, stronger than you seem, and smarter than you think." I love you.

Finally, to my amazing husband, Greg, I owe a huge debt of gratitude. I appreciate your willingness to allow me to share our story. You are my anchor, my sail and my wind. I will share your joy and sorrow till we've seen this journey through. Je t'aime, Greg.

Connect with Julie and Andria

Please visit

www.lettinggoofthestatusquo.com

for information on webinars, workshops and other products and services available to support you with your reinvention journey.

33705172R00136

Made in the USA
Middletown, DE
23 July 2016